Implementing TQM in Small & Medium-Sized Organizations

Implementing TQM in Small & Medium-Sized Organizations

A Step-by-Step Guide

Richard M. Hodgetts

American Management Association

New York • Atlanta • Boston • Chicago • Kansas City • San Francisco • Washington, D.C.
Brussels • Mexico City • Tokyo • Toronto

Library of Congress Cataloging-in-Publication Data

Hodgetts, Richard M.
    *Implementing TQM in small & medium-sized organizations: a step-by
-step guide / Richard M. Hodgetts.*
        p. cm.
    Includes bibliographical references and index.
    ISBN 0-8144-0290-9
    *1. Small business—Management—Handbooks, manuals, etc. 2. Total
quality management—Handbooks, manuals, etc.. I. Title.*
    HD62.7.H6253 1995
    658.02'2—dc20   *95-31476*
                                                          CIP

Printing number

10 9 8 7 6 5 4 3 2

To
Henry Sternlieb,
a total quality manager

Contents

Preface

The word *quality* seems to crop up in just about everything that is being written about management. Companies talk about the improved quality of their products and services by pointing to the reduction they have achieved in performance defects and customer complaints. They point to their just-in-time (or more likely just-in-case) inventory systems that now operate on a more hand-to-mouth basis than ever before. They note their ability to compete more effectively with foreign companies and proudly display charts and graphs that show reduced error rates, increased customer satisfaction, and rising profitability.

Indeed an increasing number of organizations seem to have taken quality to heart and are now prospering because of this strategic decision. Many of these are larger enterprises that can afford to bring in consultants and assign inside associates to work full time on the organization's quality initiative. But what about small businesses that lack resources to hire outside assistance to train their staff and get these companies started along the quality path? What about universities and colleges that need to provide more services than ever before, and on increasingly tight budgets? What about small health care organizations that are being caught in the cost-service squeeze and are being forced to lower their expenses in order to compete against their larger, better-financed rivals? What hope do these organizations have of maintaining their competitiveness and matching their rivals step for step?

This question occurred to me when I was conducting interviews around the country a few years ago, talking to those premier American organizations that had won Baldrige awards. These awards are given annually by the U.S. Department of Commerce to a small number of applicant companies that are judged to be meeting the highest quality standards when providing their goods and services. When I completed *Blueprints for Continuous Improvement: Lessons for the Baldrige Winners,* a briefing for the American Management Association in 1993, I decided to turn my attention to the ways in which *every* organization could improve its quality, even if it never reached the level at which it would qualify to win a Baldrige. The result of my efforts is this book, which is designed for all enterprises: business, health care, academic, and others. I have tried to emphasize the need for practicality and have assumed that the reader either wants to improve quality in his or her organization and needs some simple, easy-to-apply ideas or has already begun this quality trek and would welcome some additional insights that can be used to improve the current process. Therefore, my emphasis here is on practicality.

My initial plan was to visit small and medium-sized organizations that had total quality management (TQM) programs in operation, spend a few days with each company, and learn some of the shortcuts and solutions that were being used, and some of the pitfalls too. I intended to take this information and couple it with what I discovered as a consultant to local businesses in the Miami area, where I was helping to introduce and implement TQM programs. The result of these efforts was to be a book on TQM for small and medium-sized organizations. However, as I began gaining more experience and started lining up the businesses that I intended to visit, I learned two salient facts:

1. Many state and local governments and organizations were establishing quality awards for local companies, and these companies would be ideal targets for my inquiries.
2. Far more organizations were getting on the quality bandwagon than I had anticipated, so my choice of companies turned out to be much larger than I initially thought.

In addition, while attending quality meetings at the Coral Gables Chamber of Commerce and talking to people at other nearby chambers regarding local businesses and their TQM efforts. I became actively involved in a large TQM training program under the auspices of the Center for Management Development at Florida International University. Eventually I refocused my thinking and began contacting and visiting companies in the local area that were in the process of implementing TQM programs. At the same time I began reaching out to other states and talking to agencies that were responsible for managing that state's quality award program. From this process I gathered a wealth of information from state award winners in New York, Connecticut, Missouri, Nevada, Minnesota, New Mexico, and Florida. I also learned a great deal about what many of the other states, in the process of developing their own awards, were doing.

After months of gathering data, I carefully analyzed the information and realized that many of these organizations faced common challenges and used similar approaches in meeting them. Moreover, much of what they were doing could be emulated by just about any organization that was willing to commit the necessary time and minimal resources.

This is the first book that breaks quality into simple, applicable, and easily implementable steps. It pulls together a composite of what these organizations have done and presents them in the form of seven easy-to-understand-and-apply steps. Each step is explained in a separate chapter, which contains a worksheet designed to help the reader implement what has just been explained.

Many organizations and individuals were instrumental in providing me with the assistance needed in writing this book, and I have selected examples for each chapter of how organizations apply specific ideas. I have chosen examples that are clear and easily applicable, so that they can be easily emulated. At the same time I have tried to remain faithful to the Baldrige award criteria, which I find more and more organizations are accepting as a starting point in developing their TQM programs. Some of these criteria include customer-driven quality, an emphasis on continuous improvement, full employee participation in the TQM process, reduction in the time needed to bring new goods and services to market, and management by fact. These criteria have become so well accepted that they serve as the basis for most state and local quality awards.

How This Book Will Help You

This book will be of value to you in a number of ways. Primarily, it will help you increase your quality, develop and maintain an advantage over your competitors, and continuously improve by creating ever-better approaches. In particular, this book will help you do the following:

- Better understand what you mean by the term *quality* and learn how to use this information to develop a comprehensive, profitable, quality-driven strategy.
- Organize and develop a focus for all of your quality efforts.
- Identify specific steps for getting client feedback on how well you are doing and what else needs to be done.
- Create customer-driven strategies for satisfying client needs, now and in the future.
- Design simple, cost-effective structures for carrying out your quality effort.
- Continually get feedback from and give feedback to your organization's associates by developing an open, interactive communication system.
- Provide recognition and rewards to the associates who are contributing to the quality effort.
- Create a continuous improvement system for measuring bottom-line results.

I have written this book with one overriding question in mind: What do readers need to know so they can institute or improve their own TQM approach? I believe I have answered this question, and when you are finished reading and implementing the ideas in this book, I think you will agree. However, it is important to remember that no one book on quality management is ever sufficient to address every question or to cover every aspect of the subject. That is why I have also provided a brief annotated Bibliography at the end of the book, which will give you additional sources. By examining the Bibliography, you will be able to choose other resources that will help expand and further clarify the ideas in *Implementing TQM in Small and Medium-Sized Organizations*.

Acknowledgments

In writing this book, I have had a great deal of support and assistance. Anthony Vlamis, my acquisitions editor at AMACOM, provided both encouragement and advice regarding how to strengthen and focus the text. Don Bohl, American Management Association editor on my *Blueprints for Continuous Improvement*, helped light a "quality fire" under me.

Henry and Ed Sternlieb, Allan Sutherland, and Crystal Duxbury of the Henry Lee Company provided me a wealth of information related to total quality and the ways in which they are using it in their company. Carlos Migoya, president of First Union National Bank of Florida for Dade and Monroe Counties, made himself available to me for interviews and opened doors throughout the bank for me. John Thwing of Texaco allowed me to sit in on his TQM seminars and learn how these ideas can be used by a myriad of organizations, from banks to police departments. Alan Barraclough and Tom Land of Motorola provided copious information regarding changes in the quality area and how they are likely to affect small and medium-sized companies.

Gayle Uebelhor of the North Broward Hospital District, Karla Perez of Valley Hospital Medical Center in Las Vegas, Nevada, and Frank Fernandez of Baptist Hospital of Miami helped me better understand how TQM concepts can be used in health care organizations. Emma Lou Brent, president of the Phelps County Bank, responded to copious telephone calls, answered a wide array of questions, and provided me with information on every quality management aspect of her operation that I requested. Greg LeBlanc of Perkin-Elmer was also extremely generous with his time and support for this book. And Don Wainwright of Wainwright Industries not only answered all of my questions but was kind enough to send me a copy of his Baldrige award application, so that I could gain a better understanding of how his organization focused its TQM efforts.

Just as I was finishing the last chapter of this book and writing a section on how Wainwright Industries applied TQM, I decided to take a short coffee break and scan *The Wall Street Journal*. Imagine my surprise when the first story I turned to was an announcement from the federal government that five companies had been awarded the 1994 Baldrige: four large corporations—and Wainwright Industries!

A number of organizations provided information that I used

in this book. Since some of them are not very well known enterprises, I have included a brief description of their business as well:

Company	*Business*
American Capital Companies Shareholder Services, Inc. (ACCESS)	Transfer agent
AIL Systems, Inc.	High-technology electronics
Baptist Hospital of Miami	Health care
Blue Cross and Blue Shield of Arizona	Health insurance
Boise Cascade	Office products
Electronic Controls Company (ECCO)	Electronic components
EG&G Energy Measurements	Advanced technology products
First Union National Bank of Florida	Financial services
Folger's Coffee	Food
Group Technologies	Electronic contract manufacturing
Henry Lee Company	Food service distributor
Mayport Naval Station	Naval support
North Broward Hospital District	Health care
Perkin-Elmer	Chemical and life sciences
Phelps County Bank	Financial services
Valley Hospital Medical Center	Health care
Wainwright Industries	Precision manufacturing
Wild Oats	Natural foods and health care products
Zytec	Power supplies

Finally, I thank my colleagues at Florida International University (FIU) and other academic institutions who provided me with
quality-related materials, read parts of this manuscript and offered
substantive comments, and encouraged me in this effort: Hal

Wyman, dean of the College of Business at FIU; Gary Dessler, chairman of the Department of Management and International Business; Willabeth Jordan, director of the Center for Management Development; Anisya Thomas, FIU; Doug Smith, FIU; Fred Luthans, University of Nebraska, Lincoln; Ronald Greenwood, GMI; and Jane Gibson, Nova University.

Implementing TQM in Small & Medium-Sized Organizations

1

The Quality Revolution —And How to Be a Winner in the Battle Zones Ahead

When the total quality management (TQM) movement began in earnest in the United States during the 1980s, many organizations hurried to get on board. However, many small and medium-sized organizations felt that they either could not afford to make the necessary changes in their operations because of the high investment of time and money or they believed that the movement would not affect them and they could remain in a protected niche, shielded from competitive pressures. Both of these beliefs have proved wrong. We are in the middle of a quality revolution that is rapidly spreading across the country. Proof of this revolution was offered in the 1994 World Competitiveness Report; at the top of the list was the United States! Japan was third, a marked change from a few years earlier when the United States had fallen into fifth place and, to some, appeared to be losing its international competitive edge.

Quality has rebounded in America for a number of reasons. One, overlooked by many observers, is the grass-roots movement among small and medium-sized companies, encouraged by the recent rise in the number of state and local quality awards that are annually given to organizations throughout the country. For example, among the many are: Florida's Sterling Award, New York's Excelsior Award, and Missouri's Missouri Quality Award. And the winners are often organizations that are less than household names. For example, here are some select winners in the last few years:

Florida: Armstrong World Industries, Inc.
               Pinellas County Schools
               Mayport Naval Station
New York: Trident Tool Co.
               AIL Systems, Inc.
               Pearl River School District
Missouri: American Capital Companies Shareholder Ser-
               vices, Inc.
               Wainwright Industries
               Phelps County Bank

Who has heard of these organizations? Mostly only local residents.

Of course, there are also well-known companies that have won state awards, but the point to remember is that not all high-quality enterprises are large, nor do they have millions of dollars to spend on the development of TQM systems. Many are small and work on very tight budgets, yet they too have been successful. Simply put, the quality revolution is now involving all enterprises regardless of size and financial status. And there is one thing they all seem to have in common: similar philosophies and strategies for reaching their quality goals. This is a result of developing the right perspective.

Developing the Right Perspective

Organizations that are just beginning to think about introducing TQM programs often ask, "How do we get started?" "What are the first steps we should take?" "What should our overall game plan look like?" Enterprises that have answered these questions know the importance of developing the right perspective by looking at what they want to do and then carefully planning their strategy.

More and more of these approaches are being driven by a Baldrige criteria framework. From city halls to state governments to federal agencies, an increasing number of quality programs are being based on the U.S. government's Baldrige award criteria. In Florida and Missouri, for example, applicants for state awards are required to submit applications that show that their organization is familiar with the Baldrige criteria and can prove that the enterprise is adhering to each of the critical areas associated with this award:

- Customer satisfaction and retention
- Market share and new product development
- Product and service quality
- Productivity, operational effectiveness, and responsiveness
- Human resources performance and development
- Supplier performance and development
- Public responsibility and corporate citizenship

To make this clearer, it is worth taking a few minutes to examine the Baldrige award criteria. The quality award framework used in Missouri and presented in Exhibit 1-1 provides a good basis for this discussion.

Basic Elements

There are four basic elements in the Baldrige (and Missouri Quality Award) framework:

1. *Driver.* The senior executives who create the values, goals, and systems and guide the ongoing pursuit of customer value and organization performance improvement. Management has to lead the quality movement.
2. *Goal.* The delivery of ever-improving value to customers. This means continued striving to reduce error rates, while working to increase customer satisfaction.
3. *System.* A set of well-defined and well-designed processes for meeting customer needs. This calls for designing and implementing the necessary structure, procedures, and guidelines for achieving the desired quality goals.
4. *Measures of progress.* Measures that provide feedback and help the organization identify changes that need to be made. In this way, the enterprise is able to provide ever-better products and services to its customers.

Exhibit 1-1. Missouri Quality Award criteria framework.

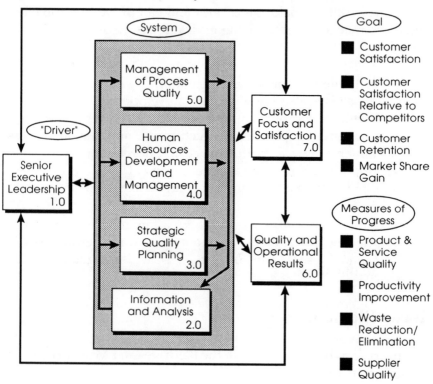

Companies applying for the Missouri Quality Award clearly understand the dynamic relationships among the driver, the systems, the goal, and the measures of progress. The organizations that were the focal point of attention in this book do also, and their actions can be tied directly to the seven areas (labeled 1.0 through 7.0) in Exhibit 1-1. These are commonly referred to as areas of excellence.

Areas of Excellence

As seen in Exhibit 1-1, senior-level management drives the quality effort. This striving will be successful only if the managers have a well-designed system in place. The outcome of this system—

customer satisfaction and operational results—lets management know how well it is doing. In turn, this feedback is useful in modifying both the leadership efforts and the system.

1. *Leadership.* The first area of excellence, leadership, addresses the senior executives' personal guidance and involvement in creating and then sustaining a customer focus and clear and visible quality values. Top-level managers provide this leadership by:

- Becoming personally involved in the quality process
- Clearly communicating the importance of quality to employees
- Constantly reviewing performance to ensure that the quality focus is maintained
- Recognizing and rewarding contributions
- Continually urging everyone to keep improving

Top management, in other words, leads the quality effort through involvement and role modeling. They don't just talk the talk; they walk it with everyone else in the organization.

2. *Information and analysis.* The organization's system is designed so that it gathers accurate information on operational performance and then carefully evaluates the data. Some of the key steps in this process are:

- Deciding the types of information to gather
- Determining how to use this information to measure progress
- Deciding how this information will be used to still improve internal operations further

3. *Strategic quality planning.* In addressing this area of excellence, the organization identifies all key quality and operational performance requirements and then integrates them into an overall plan. This work encompasses:

- Creating a plan that addresses the quality objectives that are most important to the customer

- Focusing on the objectives that will create defect-free products
- Developing a rapid response to customer needs
- Determining how to reduce the time needed to provide goods and services
- Increasing productivity and holding prices at competitive levels

4. *Human resources development and management.* Management's game plan here is to make sure that everyone understands what the quality effort is all about and that they are able to play an active role in this effort. Some of the most common activities here are:

- Providing everyone with education and training
- Developing effective recognition and reward systems
- Creating initiatives that promote cooperation among management, labor, unions, and outside vendors
- Designing feedback systems that help measure employee satisfaction and chart these changes along a time continuum

5. *Management of process quality.* In this area, the enterprise looks for ways to improve quality, operational performance, and assessment—for example:

- Designing and introducing new production and delivery processes that cut product errors and improve service quality
- Developing programs with vendors that help link the organization and the supplier in a synergistic way, thus increasing quality and reducing cost
- Designing quality assessment systems for evaluating the overall results and ensuring continuous improvement in the process

6. *Quality and operational results.* In keeping track of progress, primary attention is given to facts: revenues, costs, percentages, and ratios, with anecdotal data such as stories given little value. It's not enough to be providing higher-quality goods and services;

the company must prove it objectively. There are a number of ways that this is typically done, including:

- Conducting customer surveys
- Comparing current quality levels with those of the past in order to show improvement
- Comparing current quality levels with those of similar organizations, industry leaders, and other appropriate benchmarks

7. *Customer focus and satisfaction.* In addressing this area of excellence, the enterprise examines its relationship with the customers in order to ensure that client needs are being met. Some of the steps in this process include:

- Identifying specific customer groups or market niches
- Soliciting feedback regarding what each group or niche would like, both now and over the next three to five years
- Identifying the steps that will have to be taken to meet these current and future needs
- Evaluating customer complaints and developing a response system for handling these issues
- Identifying the current level and trend of customer satisfaction as measured by surveys and other forms of feedback
- Comparing customer satisfaction results and trends with those of similar organizations

The following chapters address these seven areas of excellence and detail ways in which successful companies deal with each. Before doing this, however, it is important to examine the core values and concepts that form the basis for most quality efforts. These are a reflection of the seven areas of excellence, but they warrant individual consideration because they expand that explanation and add elements that are important to understanding how to achieve quality in an efficient way.

Core Values and Concepts

There are ten core values and concepts that create the basis for quality awards. Collectively they provide a series of critical guidelines that ultimately dictate the success of the organization's quality effort.

1. *Customer-driven quality.* Quality is judged by the customer, so all product and service efforts are designed to contribute value to the customer and lead to buyer satisfaction. When buyers are satisfied, they will prefer the company's goods and services over those of others. In achieving this core value, some of the most common objectives include:

- Building trust, confidence, and loyalty by not just meeting customer requirements but going the extra mile
- Differentiating the goods and services from those of the competition
- Leaving the customer not just satisfied but delighted

2. *Leadership.* All senior leaders in the organization must create a customer orientation. They must set clear and visible quality values and have high expectations. These values and expectations are reinforced by their substantial personal commitment. These leaders must serve as role models throughout the organization, thus reinforcing the quality values at all levels.

3. *Continuous improvement.* It is not enough for an organization to be better than it was previously; it needs to strive for continuous improvement. Among the ways that this can be done are encouraging creativity, maintaining a continuous improvement environment, and recognizing and rewarding associates for doing a good job. The last way is particularly important because in continuous improvement, what gets rewarded gets done.

4. *Associate participation and development.* Associates in award-winning organizations are closely involved in the TQM process, and their support and contribution are critical to the overall effort. These companies invest in associate development through education, training, and opportunities for continuing growth. For their part, associates learn how to align their efforts with the company's direction by accepting new ideas and being willing to upgrade and improve their skills.

5. *Fast response.* Success in competitive markets increasingly demands that the time between creation of new goods and their

delivery to the customer be reduced. Faster and more flexible response to customers is becoming an ever more critical requirement. Successful enterprises achieve fast response by simplifying work procedures and processes, while maintaining time and quality standards.

6. *Design quality and prevention.* Award-winning organizations emphasize design quality by doing things right the first time. One of the key rules they follow is, "Prevention rather than detection." It is more productive to sidestep mistakes than to deal with them, regardless of the organization's efficiency. By building quality into products and services in the production process, the enterprise reduces the costs of correcting problems that occur downstream.

7. *Long-range outlook.* In achieving quality and market leadership, organizations look to the future and are willing to make long-term commitments to all stakeholders: customers, employees, suppliers, stockholders, the public, and the community. To achieve a long-range outlook, enterprises must determine or anticipate many types of changes:

- Customer expectations of products and services
- Technological development
- Changing customer segments
- Evolving regulatory requirements
- Community and societal expectations
- Strategic moves by competitors

Additionally, a major part of the long-term commitment is to develop employees and suppliers, fulfill public responsibilities, and serve as a corporate citizenship role model.

8. *Management by fact.* Many organizations rely on anecdotal references, such as stories or comments from customers, to indicate how well they are doing (or not doing), but management by fact requires the use of specific, measurable data. The TQM feedback system is built on objective data and analysis—for example, customer surveys, error rates, and costs, all of which are quantitative and can be charted over time. Most of this information can be gathered simply and easily, with no need for sophisticated mathematical tools and techniques. When it has this information, the

company is in a position to determine quickly how well it is doing, compare its performance to that of competitive or benchmarked companies, and decide the action that is now warranted.

9. *Partnership development.* Successful organizations build internal and external partnerships to help them accomplish their overall goals. Examples of internal partnerships are better labor-management cooperation, employee development, cross-training, and the creation of high-performance work teams. External partnerships include cooperation with customers, suppliers, and other outside organizations. An increasingly important external relationship is the strategic partnership or alliance, which can offer entry into new markets or a basis for the creation of new products or services. Such an arrangement also permits the blending of the organization's core competencies or leadership capabilities with the complementary strengths and capabilities of the partner, thereby enhancing overall speed and flexibility.

10. *Corporate responsibility and citizenship.* Successful organizations address their responsibility and citizenship. Corporate responsibility refers to the basic expectations of the enterprise, including business ethics and protection of public health, safety, and the environment. Corporate citizenship refers to leadership and support of publicly important purposes, such as education, environmental excellence, improved industry and business practices, and the sharing of nonproprietary quality-related information. Leadership as a corporate citizen also entails the influencing of other organizations, private and public, to partner for these purposes.

These core values and concepts are critical to the success of every TQM effort. They are integrated into all of the chapters that follow.

Objectives of This Book

This book has four primary objectives, all incorporated into each chapter:

1. To provide a series of understandable, implementable TQM ideas that can be adapted by any organization, private or public, and can be employed at all levels of the structure.
2. To reinforce these ideas with practical illustrations and examples, so that the linkage joining theory (why something is being done), process (how it is being done), and practice (what is being done) is clear.
3. To offer a series of steps and illustrations that can be implemented without spending a great deal of money on equipment and materials (although it certainly will take a substantial investment of time if it is to be done correctly).
4. To reinforce these ideas through the use of worksheets, located in each chapter, which have been specifically designed to help carry out each step in the quality process.

In addressing these objectives, I have relied heavily on the Baldrige criteria to help focus the data I gathered from the organizations in this study. The areas I stress are of critical importance, regardless of the enterprise's vision or mission. They are:

• Customer and employee satisfaction
• Data collection
• Employee training
• Design of the structure
• Provision of recognition and rewards
• Development of a system for continuous improvement

Throughout the book I have placed primary attention on presenting the ideas and suggestions that can be most profitably applied. In doing so, I have relied on ten guidelines which collectively spell

P-R-O-F-I-T-A-B-L-E

1. *Practical.* The ideas must be applicable to the needs of the organization and not based solely on theory.
2. *Results oriented.* The ideas have to bring about some useful outcomes.

3. *Original.* The applications have to be designed so that they meet the unique needs of the enterprise.
4. *Focused.* The suggestions have to be directed toward a specific area so that their purpose is clear.
5. *Implementable.* It must be possible to carry out these ideas within the time and cost constraints of the organization.
6. *Timely.* It must be possible to apply these ideas as they are needed; they cannot require inordinate amounts of time and effort.
7. *Adaptable.* The ideas must be able to be modified so that they fit the specific and ever-changing needs of the organization.
8. *Broadly based.* Everyone in the organization must be able to participate in at least some part of the TQM effort.
9. *Long term.* The ideas must be sustainable through some system such as continuous improvement, thus ensuring that the organization does not lose its quality focus after a few years of success.
10. *Efficient.* The TQM concepts must result in working better, faster, and/or less expensively, depending on the needs of the customer.

These P-R-O-F-I-T-A-B-L-E guidelines help reinforce a TQM idea that is worth keeping in mind as you read this book:

> In many cases there is an *inverse* relationship between quality and cost.

This means that as quality goes up, costs come down. (It may *seem* that just the opposite should occur, but let me assure you that it usually does not.) Exhibit 1-2 provides an example of Motorola's old assumption regarding the relationship between cost and quality. A close look at the exhibit helps explain why many organizations in the past did not attempt to drive up quality: The cost was too high. Notice that as the number of failures approaches zero, the cost of achieving this objective becomes extremely high. It is no wonder that many organizations in the past felt that TQM was too costly and were happy to settle for quality that was "good enough."

Exhibit 1-2. Motorola's old assumption regarding the relationship between cost and quality.

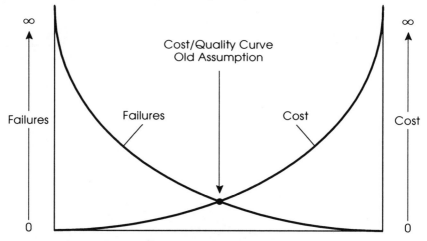

Source: Motorola quality briefing. Used by permission.

   Today we know that improving quality can drive down costs. This concept is illustrated in Exhibit 1-3, where the five cost curves (3 sigma through 7 sigma) represent declining failure rates. As engineers know, 3 sigma is a statistical notation that represents 66,810 errors per 1 million; 4 sigma is 6,210 errors per million; 5 sigma is 233 errors per million; 6 sigma is 3.4 errors per million; and 7 sigma is virtually errorless performance. By decreasing the error rate, say, from 3 sigma (6.68 percent) to 6 sigma (0.00034 percent) a company eliminates approximately 66,806 mistakes. How much money does this save the organization? It's hard to say, but one thing is certain: All of the time and money that would have had to be spent correcting these mistakes would, for all intents and purposes, be saved, and the loss of customer satisfaction and repeat business stemming from these mistakes would be eliminated. A good way of thinking of this issue is to answer the question: *How much time and money would my organization save if we did not make mistakes?* So although the cost of training associates in TQM concepts and going up the learning curve will take time and money, these expenses are often more than offset by the savings that are effected. This is one of the primary reasons for introducing TQM programs: They save money. They are P-R-O-F-I-T-A-B-L-E!

Exhibit 1-3. Motorola's research results regarding the relationship between cost and quality.

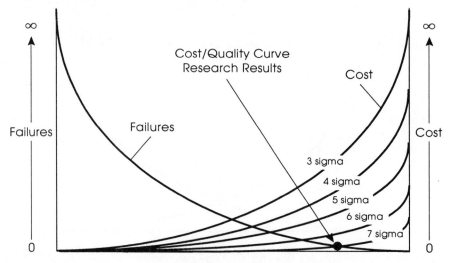

Source: Motorola quality briefing. Used by permission.

What I Learned

As I noted in the Preface, I contacted, visited, and received TQM materials for a wide number and array of organizations. Of the thirty companies on which I initially focused my efforts, I drew materials from nineteen to use as the basis for this book. But from all of this information, I found that seven steps were universally followed by all of these organizations. These steps form the basis for this book. They are:

1. *Develop a quality focus by creating a vision and/or mission statement.* This step provides the point of departure. When it is not carried out first, the quality effort often flounders because the organization is not sure where to go.
2. *Identify customer needs.* This step is carried out by gathering information from both internal customers (employees) and external customers (buyers) through such approaches as surveys and interviews.

3. *Design an organization structure that helps implement a quality-driven strategy.* An individual or group must oversee the TQM effort and ensure that the momentum is not lost.
4. *Train the associates in the necessary tools and techniques,* such as checksheets, Pareto charts, cause-and-effect diagrams, and brainstorming. Be sure to use *only* the tools that are useful to your organization. Forget the rest.
5. *Give feedback to and get feedback from both internal and external customers.* Design this feedback in a way that meets the unique needs of customers.
6. *Develop an effective recognition and reward system* that associates feel is motivational.
7. *Create the necessary climate for maintaining continuous improvement efforts,* including reviewing all previous guidelines and using this information to help keep the quality momentum.

In the chapters that follow, I develop each of these seven ideas in depth. In each case, I have tried to make the material interesting and applicable. If you follow the suggestions that follow the chapter material, I am certain that you will understand why I have titled this book *Implementing TQM in Small and Medium-Sized Organizations.* So come with me now as we begin our quality journey by examining how to develop a quality focus.

2

Develop a Focus—
Know Where You're Going,
and Then Sound
the Drums

One of the companies I studied for this book is Zytec, a small power supply business in Minnesota. Zytec is not just a state award winner but a Baldrige winner and a world-class manufacturer. How did such a small (and pretty much unknown) company become so good? The same way that many other small and intermediate-sized companies have. It faced a crisis that threatened to shut it down. The company had to develop a quality focus and become increasingly more competitive—or go bankrupt. Its story is not unique. Consider the case of Globe Metallurgical, a small steel company with facilities in Ohio and Alabama.

Globe was confronted with strong competition and knew that it had to lower costs and increase efficiency or go out of business. Top management got training in TQM and started to implement many of these ideas—and none too soon. The union, unable to reach a satisfactory contract with the company, suddenly walked out. As a result, management and a small group of hourly workers found themselves running the plant for the next two years. Implementing many of the TQM ideas they learned, and picking up a lot more through on-the-job applications, Globe's management and workers streamlined operations and sharply increased productivity. In the seven-year period that began when the company decided to introduce a TQM-driven strategy and ended with the introduction of new computer technology into the plants, Globe's sales increased by 47 percent, total employment dropped by 42 percent, international sales went up by 1900 percent, and the company had a 90 percent capacity utilization rate, compared to 40 percent for the rest of the industry.

There are hundreds of similar stories all over America, for in the past decade, an increasing number of small and medium-sized companies have come to realize that quality is no longer an option. Today it's quality or else!

If your organization has not yet reached the crisis point, where quality changes must be quickly introduced, you have some breathing room—but not much. Every day more and more small and medium-sized enterprises are introducing TQM ideas into their operations. The time for you to start is now, and the place to begin is by developing a focus or central point to which you can direct your quality efforts. Follow these four simple steps:

First	Ask the right questions, so you can learn what quality is all about and how you can become more quality-focused in terms of your customers, competitors, and associates.
Second	Gather this information, and analyze it so you are able to answer key questions: How can you improve your quality? Who are your customers, and what do you need to do to keep their business? Who are your competitors, and how can you counter their efforts? What do you need to do to keep your employees loyal and productive? How can you improve the general public's perception of your organization? Why are you in business?
Third	Look at the vision, mission, statement of purpose, and objectives of other successful organizations, including competitors, and use this information to help you decide how to focus your own organization's quality efforts.
Fourth	Create your own quality focus statement, no matter how brief or preliminary it is. Then use this initial effort as a basis for formulating a more sharply focused, more detailed statement that is unique to your operation.

Ask the *Right* Questions

The first step in creating a total quality–driven organization is to decide what you want to do. Obviously you hope to increase the quality of your offerings. However, what specifically are you going to do? When asked this question, most owner-managers or senior-level personnel provide answers such as these:

> We're going to make a better product.

> We're going to find out what our customer wants, and we're going to go out of our way to accommodate this individual.

> We're going to achieve total customer satisfaction.

> We're going to become the number one company in our local market.

> We're going to offer the best goods and services at competitive prices.

While useful in most cases, these comments are knee-jerk reactions because management does not know for sure what it is going to do. All management knows is that things have to be done differently if quality is to be increased.

The best way to focus a quality effort is by asking the *right* questions. These questions should focus on four main areas: (1) what quality is all about, (2) what customers currently want and what they are likely to want in the future, (3) what the competition is doing, and (4) the changes that the business has to consider making if it is going to become (or remain) profitable. The specific questions to ask are provided in the following worksheet, and they should be answered by both you and your key associates. (Make some copies of the worksheet for distribution.) Then set a meeting time for discussing the responses.

Quality and Us

Read and answer or complete each of the following questions. Do not spend a great deal of time on each, since general impressions or ideas are more important than your ability to write a refined or detailed formal answer. Try to answer all twelve questions within 60 minutes.

1. Complete the following statement: In this organization, when we talk about improving quality we mean . . .

2. Complete the following statement: If I could make just one change to improve quality in this organization, it would be . . .

3. Complete the following statment: The main reason that customers buy from us is . . .

4. If customers were asked to list the things they like *best* about doing business with us, what would they say? List three to five responses.

5. If customers were asked to list the things they liked *least* about doing business with us, what would they say? List three to five responses.

6. Over the past three years, how have customer demands changed? Identify three changes.

7. How are customer demands likely to change over the next two years? Identify three developments that you believe are most likely to occur.

8. Who are our major competitors? Identify them, and explain what makes them so competitive.

9. What do associates like *most* about working here? List three to five things.

10. What do associates like *least* about working here? List three to five things.

11. How is our organization viewed by outsiders? When our name is mentioned, what are some things people think or say about us?

12. The main reason(s) we are in business is (are):

Record the Responses and Seek Consensus

The purpose of the worksheet you just completed is to provide you with a basis for focusing on quality. In particular, the questions are designed to help you identify what quality is all about and how you can become more quality-focused in terms of your customers, your competitors, and your associates. As you review the worksheet answers, have one of the group members write down the responses. If you have a flipchart, put each answer on an individual sheet and tape the sheets on the walls of the room so that everyone can clearly see and review the various responses. Here are the questions along with guidelines for addressing each.

1. **Complete the following statement: In this organization when we talk about improving quality we mean . . .**

   This answer will help you identify exactly what you mean by the word *quality*. It also helps focus the discussion because once people have answered this question, it is easier to keep referring back to quality and using the term to direct the discussion. After you have written down the responses, get everyone to work together in creating a definition of quality by completing this sentence: "Quality is. . . ."

2. **Complete the following statement: If I could make just one change to improve quality in this organization, it would be . . .**

   The purpose of this question is to identify some of the changes that should be considered during the early stages of the quality effort. Typically the answers to this question fit into one of three categories: (a) changes that are regarded as critical, (b) changes that are easiest to make, or (c) changes that directly affect the operation of the respondent's unit or department. In any event, when examining these responses, look for those that are most important and those that are easiest to implement. The reason is that you eventually will have to incorporate critical changes into your overall TQM plan, but in getting things off the ground, it is often best to start with a simple change that can be quickly implemented. As the momentum for quality changes increases, you can turn to more important changes that will require greater time and effort.

3. **Complete the following statement: The main reason that customers buy from us is . . .**

This answer helps you identify what company associates regard as the organization's major strength or selling point. The answer is important in focusing the quality effort because you need to find out what you are doing best and then create a strategy for continuing to build on this strength. The answer is also important because after you poll your customers (a step discussed in the next chapter), you can compare their responses to the one(s) you received to this question.

4. **If customers were asked to list the things they like *best* about doing business with us, what would they say? List three to five responses.**

This question is a follow-on to the previous one and helps identify the perceptions of your associates regarding customer satisfaction. It is also useful in identifying perceived patterns of strengths. For example, you may find that most of your staff feel that your product line selection is viewed postively by customers, who also like the fact that you are continually introducing new products. The answers also provide a basis for comparisons with responses from customer surveys that ask similar questions.

5. **If customers were asked to list the things they liked *least* about doing business with us, what would they say? List three to five responses.**

This question is the reverse of the previous one and is designed to identify areas where employees feel the organization does not do a good job. Some of these responses may not surprise you and may not need to be addressed. For example, if you are a supplier of high-quality office furniture, it is likely that your prices are high. So customers may say that they do not like these prices, but you are not going to lower them in order to address this concern because that will change your image and could have a negative impact on customer loyalty. On the other hand, there are likely to be a number of answers that help highlight quality-related errors that need to be corrected. For example, associates may feel that customers have to wait too long for service because there are not sufficient sales associates to serve them.

6. **Over the past three years, how have customer demands changed? Identify three changes.**

   The objective of this question is to help identify the need for change. For example, many companies are finding that customers have become more demanding, have greater options regarding what to buy and where to buy it, and are more knowledgeable regarding what they need and how much they should pay for it. As a result, most organizations have found that they must provide better-quality goods and services today than they did in the recent past. Regardless of what you find, follow up the results by asking, "Why have demands changed?" and list the responses.

7. **How are customer demands likely to change over the next two years? Identify three developments that you believe are most likely to occur.**

   This question builds on the previous one. Some of the responses are likely to be mere extensions of what the company is doing now. For example, if prices have come down 15 percent in the past two years, the associates may say that there will continue to be pressure to lower prices even more. This analysis, however, is not sufficiently savvy; anyone can use extrapolation to conclude that the future will be more of the past. Respondents must also answer the question: What new developments will occur that are *not* now being offered? This is a more difficult question; it forces the employees to face the fact that some of the changes that are on the horizon will be new and even threatening because they will change the way the company currently does business. In getting a better handle on this line of analysis, a good place to start is by reviewing the list of changes in customer demands that have occurred over the past three years and asking, "How many of these were we able to predict and quickly address, and how many of them required us to make changes in the way we were doing business?" This inquiry forces the respondents to admit that some changes were not adequately forecasted, and as recently as a few years ago the company was already scrambling to make changes in order to remain competitive.

8. **Who are our major competitors? Identify them, and explain what makes them so competitive.**

   The objective of this question is to address competitive forces and to pinpoint some of the reasons for the success of these companies. Some of the answers to this question can be used in identifying core competencies that are critical to success. Other answers will help highlight the current and future strategies of the competition. More important, however, the answers will tell you who is doing best, and why. Based on this information, you should be able to identify the actions your company will have to take if it wants to remain competitive. It is also possible to use this competitive analysis to identify market niches that are not being well served or are likely to emerge and could prove profitable for you. Most important, this question can help you identify the gap between what you are doing now and what you must do in the future. For example, you may find that your competitors fill orders faster than you do or offer the same output at a lower price. These conclusions point to strategies that you must consider: How can you reduce cycle time? How can you lower cost without reducing quality?

9. **What do associates like *most* about working here? List three to five things.**

   This question is designed to focus on internal customers. Many small and medium-sized organizations tend to overlook the fact that they have two customers: external customers, who buy the good or service that is being produced, and internal customers, who participate in producing the output that is being sold. The answers to this question can serve as a basis for developing additional employee-focused programs. For example, many small and medium-sized companies find that their associates like the fact that they are empowered to make decisions and handle problems without approval from above on everything. Another common response is that they feel like members of a small family because they know the owners and can interact with them daily. These operations are often run on a more relaxed, less bureaucratic basis, and this is an attractive feature.

10. What do associates like *least* about working here? List three to five things.

This question is often more important than the previous one because small and medium-sized companies sometimes fail to tap the full potential of their employees. One reason stems from their tendency to overcontrol operations. They fall into what is called the "85/15 rule of quality": 85 percent of quality-related problems are caused by rules, policies, procedures, and other administrative directives, and 15 percent of the problems are caused by the people. For example, when a customer wants to return merchandise but has lost the receipt and company rules require proof of purchase, the salesperson will refuse the request. It's not uncommon that the angry buyer will refuse to do business with the company in the future. This situation could be avoided if the salesperson has some leeway regarding how to handle the situation.

A similar example is provided by companies that set specific closing times such as 7 P.M. and refuse to allow customers to enter the store and purchase products after this time. A more flexible arrangement, impossible when company rules and regulations forbid it, would allow the store to accommodate the customer and add profit to the company's bottom line. When analyzing what people like least about the company, many employees will identify these self-defeating regulations. You can use this information to reevaluate and change some of the rules.

Another common complaint is poor supervision. This useful information provides a basis for deciding how to retrain employees and improve their overall effectiveness. In many small businesses, the owner-manager can often work more closely with these individuals or assign more effective managers to work with them and provide guidance and experience. In medium-sized companies, more formal training is often used to complement this process.

Still another common complaint revolves around pay scales and other forms of compensation. In dealing with these matters, there are a number of alternatives, including: (1) keeping everyone apprised of company revenues and profits so that they know you cannot afford to pay more; or (2) introducing a form of productivity payment plan in which the associates are rewarded for increases in profit through some profit-sharing arrangement. In either case, by becoming aware of the associates' concern, you are able to develop a strategy for dealing with it.

11. How is our organization viewed by outsiders? When our name is mentioned, what are some things people think or say about us?

A large percentage of quality is perceived. If people think you are doing a good job, they will tell their friends that they like doing business with you. If they believe your product is inferior or your associates are discourteous, they will pass along this information. The point to remember is that what people think of your business's quality is sometimes more important than the actual quality you provide. Moreover, typically there is a lag between people's perception and actuality. For example, if you run a small restaurant and feedback from your customers reveals that they would like faster food service, you can analyze the food delivery process and see where time could be eliminated. If you did manage to cut service time by 25 percent, would customers like this? Sure. But it might take a couple of months before they became aware of what you had done and you began getting credit for the better service. Conversely, if your service time increased and customers began to feel that they were waiting far too long for their food, it would take a while before your reputation for slow service became well known. So because of this lag between the time that quality changes and customers' awareness of it, perception is important. You need to know how people feel about your business. The fact that they may have misconceptions is *not* the issue. When you learn what they believe, you can work on changing their perceptions.

12. The main reason(s) we are in business is (are):

This question helps bring together company purpose and the role that quality can play in achieving this purpose. A typical response is that the company is in business to make a profit by serving a particular customer base. Certainly, the answer should include consideration of both profits and customers. Additionally, it is likely that attention will be given to the company's responsibility to its associates and to the community. These comments help pinpoint some of the company's constituency groups: customers, associates, managers, owners, the community. Once these groups have been identified, you are in a position to ask: What do we need to do for each of these groups in order to meet our responsibilities to them? The answer feeds back into the other responses and provides a basis for tying together all of the information you have gathered.

When you look at the overall responses and begin pulling everything together, you should be able to answer the following six quality-related questions:

1. What will you have to do to provide increased quality of goods and services?
2. Who are your customers, and what are you going to have to do in order to keep their business and possibly expand your customer base?
3. Who are your competitors, and what are you going to have to do to provide quality that is at least as good as theirs?
4. What do you need to do to ensure that your associates remain loyal, productive members of the organization?
5. How does the general public view your enterprise, and what can you do to improve this perception?
6. What are the main reasons that you are in business?

Answers to these questions will help focus your quality effort. However, it is often difficult to pull everything together and decide what you want to do, especially if this is your first effort at creating a quality-driven organization. You need to think more about the answers, talk to people in your organization about what all of it means, and begin getting everyone involved in the discussion. The objective of these efforts should be to answer questions specifically—for example, What is our mission or vision? Where are we going? What are our responsibilities to all of our constituency groups? Are there any basic principles or guidelines that we should make part of our operating philosophy?

At first, these questions may not make much sense. However, there is a way out of this quandary. By looking at what award-winning companies have done and using their approaches as a guide, you can use the responses to develop your own quality focus.

Look At What Others Have to Say

The following examples are all focus oriented and show a number of ways of directing the quality effort. Some of these organizations have identified a vision and/or mission; others have defined a purpose or objective. I have presented these in three categories beginning with the simplest, most direct statements and then moving on to longer, more detailed descriptions. As you read, note the style of presentation and identify those that appear to be closest to what would be best for you in focusing your own TQM efforts. They will provide you a starting point for creating your own quality vision, mission, and objectives.

Say It Simply

Some quality award winners come right to the point. Here are some succinct examples taken directly from company sources:

Group Technologies (mission):
Never lose a customer.

Zytec (vision):
Provide unsurpassed quality, service, and value.

Folger's Coffee (objective):
Improve consumer and customer satisfaction.

American Capital Companies Shareholder Services Inc. (mission):
Service is our *ONLY* product. We do it *RIGHT!* We do it RIGHT NOW!

Wild Oats (statement of purpose):
We are here to provide our customers with the best selection of whole foods and health-care products with an attitude of friendliness, eagerness to serve and readiness to educate. We are committed to making our store a pleasant place to shop and work, and to be an active, responsible contributor to the lives of our staff, customers, and community.

North Broward Hospital District (mission):
The mission of the North Broward Hospital District is to provide an integrated system of healthcare, in partnership with the community, which measurably improves the health status of the population we serve, emphasizing the highest level of satisfaction, positive clinical outcomes, and financial responsibility.

Some companies provide an explanation of what they stand for and how their mission is related to this. The result is a somewhat longer statement but one that clearly focuses the company's quality efforts. Here is an example:

AIL Systems Inc. (mission):
AIL Systems, Inc. is a leading systems integrator and producer of high-technology electronic products for defense and commercial applications. Our mission is to meet or exceed the requirements and expectations of our customers with affordable products and services, which are distinguished by their quality and innovation. The sustaining philosophy of our company is to continuously strive for higher levels of excellence in every aspect of individual and corporate performance.

Or Consider Developing a More Comprehensive Statement

Some of the companies I studied prefer a more comprehensive focus and tie their vision or mission statement to specific constituency groups. The value of this approach is that it helps the organization reaffirm its internal and external customer base. In other cases, the organization has chosen its most important constituency groups and created a vision statement for each. Here is one example:

> *First Union National Bank of Florida (Dade County vision statement):*
>
> *With Respect to Employees:*
> An organization that fosters excellence, respects diversity and provides an environment where the employees feel empowered, motivated, valued, and rewarded.
>
> *With Respect to Customers:*
> An organization whose highly satisfied customer base relies on us exclusively for all of their financial needs.
>
> *With Respect to the Community:*
> An organization that conducts business with a dedication to the highest ethical standards; provides financial support that stimulates development throughout our community and improves the quality of life; and encourages employee participation in community improvement activities.

Another approach is to write a mission statement and then follow with goals and responsibilities. The Wild Oats company notes that "a vision without a task is but a dream." To make this vision come true, the company has defined an overriding goal and identified four areas of responsibility. The company states it this way:

> Our goal is to manage and grow our business around what we call our "Four Areas of Responsibility." As a progressive company, we feel that it is essential to our success that we balance and nurture these sometimes conflicting areas of concern. They are:
>
> **Responsibility to Our Customers**
>
> Provide excellent service and quality product at a competitive price. Educate and inform our customers about

issues that affect their lives. Guarantee 100% satisfaction and be receptive to our customers' changing needs.

Responsibility to Our Staff

Provide competitive salaries, excellent benefits, and educational opportunities. Promote open communication and an opportunity to advance. Provide a positive work experience.

Responsibility to Our Community

Be actively involved personally and financially in the local communities that have supported our success.

Responsibility to Our Bottom Line

To yield superior profits that enable us to constantly improve and expand responsibly.

WE FIRMLY BELIEVE THAT OUR 4 AREAS OF RESPONSIBILITY MUST BE KEPT IN BALANCE; ONE CANNOT OVERSHADOW ANOTHER. AS WE GROW AND BECOME MORE PROFITABLE, OUR GOAL IS TO GIVE EACH OF THESE AREAS EQUAL ATTENTION.

Or Combine Mission, Vision, Objectives, and/or Principles

In some cases award-winning organizations have carefully thought through their quality approach and formulated detailed, and somewhat comprehensive, statements that clearly enunciate what they stand for and what they intend to do. Some have developed supporting principles that serve as a foundation for the entire effort. Examples are provided in Exhibits 2-1 through 2-4. As you study these examples, watch for specific ideas that you can incorporate into your own statement of mission or focus.

Bear in mind that the organizations developed these statements over time. At first, most enterprises have very short, well-directed statements such as, "Our goal is a satisfied customer" or "We aren't pleased with our service unless you are." As they get

Exhibit 2-1. EG&G Energy Measurements mission statement.

Our challenge is to fulfill, through management commitment and employee involvement, our responsibility to customers, fellow employees, communities, and suppliers. To this end, we:

- Empower our employees to use Total Quality Management methods to institute continuous improvement in our processes.
- Use innovative scientific and engineering methods to provide products and services which fully and economically meet our customers' requirements.
- Conduct our work in a manner that protects the environment and ensures public safety through community involvement, employee training, and compliance with the letter and spirit of applicable laws and regulations.
- Participate in educational, business, civic, and charitable activities as an active, involved community member.

Our commitment is to positively address the changes influencing our business, provide rewarding and challenging work, afford opportunities for employee development, recognize performance, and capitalize on opportunities for growth and continued success.

Our dedication is to the future . . . built upon the special values and traditions of our past; guided by legal, ethical, and moral standards; and driven by our commitment to excellence and continuous improvement in all we do.

Courtesy: EG&G Energy Measurements.

further into the quality effort and begin identifying who their customers really are and what these individuals want, they begin expanding their initial statements and including more philosophical and value-laden beliefs. So use the information in Exhibits 2-1 through 2-4 as food for thought and analysis.

Create Your Own Unique Focus

It's time for you to take the first step in creating your own quality focus statement: a mission statement, a vision, an objective, or simply a sentence that sets forth the quality message your organization wants to convey to its customers. This first effort is likely to need more work later, but the important thing is to put something on

Exhibit 2-2. Valley Hospital Medical Center mission and principles.

Our mission statement is to achieve long-term growth and success by providing healthcare services that:

Patients recommend to their family and friends,
Physicians prefer for their patients,
Purchasers select for their clients, and
Employees are proud of.

The hospital is committed to realizing this mission through the following principles:

Service Excellence. We will provide timely, professional, effective and efficient service to all of our customer groups.

Continuous Improvement in Measurable Ways. We will identify the key needs of our customers, assess how well we meet those needs, continuously improve our services, and measure our progress.

Employee Development. We understand that the professionalism and drive of our people are the most important factors in the quality of the service Valley Hospital Medical Center provides. We will hire talented people, increase their skills through training and experience, and provide opportunities for personal and professional growth within the company.

Ethical and Fair Treatment of All. We are committed to forming relationships of fairness and trust with our patients, our physicians, purchasers of our services, and our employees. We will conduct business according to the highest ethical standards.

Teamwork. We will work together to provide ever-improving customer service. This team approach to our work will supersede traditional departmental organization and create a true customer focus. People at all levels of the organization will participate in decision-making and process improvement.

Innovation in Service Delivery. We will invest in the development of new and better ways of delivering our services.

Compassion. We will never lose sight of the fact that we provide care and comfort to people in need. The patients and families that rely upon us are fellow human beings, and will receive respectful and dignified treatment from all of our people at all times.

Courtesy: Valley Hospital Medical Center.

Exhibit 2-3. Mayport Naval Station mission, vision, and guiding principles.

MISSION

To provide the best service in the Navy supporting all aviation, afloat and shore-based forces, improving the quality of life for everyone through a total commitment to excellence.

VISION

Our vision is a more responsive Naval Station, committed to QUALITY INNOVATION and CONTINUOUS IMPROVEMENT. We will lead the way into the future with:

- Quality leadership in all areas of our operations
- A well-trained, dedicated and motivated workforce
- Enhanced quality of service for all customers
- Full and rapid integration of new technologies and ideas
- A Total Quality working and living environment for all of our people
- An understanding and helpful relationship with our neighbors

GUIDING PRINCIPLES

WE:
- value the creativity and contributions of our workforce
- safeguard people, resources and the environment
- lead by example
- treat people with dignity and respect
- accomplish our mission through teamwork
- are never satisfied with the status quo
- are innovative

WE ARE COMMITTED TO:
- honesty, integrity and the highest standards of moral and ethical conduct
- equal opportunity for all
- rapid, professional, safe, responsive action in support of mission
- courteous customer service
- efficient use of manpower, facilities and equipment

- a thorough approach to security for the Naval Station and our tenants
- education and training
- strong community relations by being a trusted neighbor
- the welfare, dignity and morale of our workforce
- taking care of the Navy family

Source: Mayport Naval Station.

paper. You can always revise it. Also remember to draw on the information you have gathered from the worksheet earlier in this chapter, and, unless you want to do it personally, appoint a team of individuals who participated in answering the worksheet questions to work up the first draft of the quality statement. Begin by noting your ideas for each of the areas that I have set forth in the following worksheet and then try to combine them into an overall quality statement (the final section of the worksheet) that will serve as a working document.

Your Quality Focus

What is your vision? Describe it.

What is the mission of your organization? State it in 100 words or fewer.

Exhibit 2-4. Boise Cascade's company statement.

OUR TOTAL QUALITY COMMITMENT

To continuously make improvements that will enable us to anticipate, understand, and fulfill both internal and external customer expectations so that the company becomes the preferred supplier of each of our customers.

TOTAL QUALITY PRINCIPLES

LEADERSHIP: Management will provide the leadership, role models, and participation necessary to achieve Total Quality.

CULTURE: Respect for people and their ability to contribute to Total Quality is critical. By implementing the values, beliefs, and principles articulated in Directions for Boise Cascade, we will create a corporate culture that helps us to achieve Total Quality.

CUSTOMERS: Systematic and frequent feedback regarding our products and services from both internal and external customers will help enable us to anticipate, understand, and fulfill customer expectations.

SUPPLIERS: We will insist that our suppliers become partners in our Total Quality Commitment. We will work together to define mutual expectations for products and services and will provide our suppliers with the feedback necessary for continuous improvement.

PROCESS IMPROVEMENT METHODS AND RESULTS: Quality measurements and standards should be developed for all products, services, and processes to support continuous improvement in Total Quality. Continuous improvement will be accomplished by the use of problem solving and statistical methods.

RESOURCES: Our number-one tool is the ingenuity of our employees. In addition, over time, the company will provide sufficient resources—time, training, staffing, and capital—to empower our employees to achieve Total Quality.

BUSINESS PLANNING: We will involve employees, customers, and suppliers in the business planning process. Planning for and reviewing our progress toward achieving Total Quality will become an integrated part of our business planning and review processes.

COMMUNICATION: Each of us will demonstrate the importance of Total Quality to all of our audiences—other employees, customers, suppliers, shareholders, and communities—through actions as well as words.

RECOGNITION: We will celebrate progress and goal accomplishment by using many forms of recognition. Individual and team performance standards will focus on quality, productivity, and continuous improvement.

Courtesy: Boise Cascade Corporation.

What are the key objectives you are pursuing?

What responsibilities will have to be assumed by the company and its associates?

What guiding principles will help you reach your overall vision, mission, and objectives?

What is your quality statement? Put it into one or two well-chosen sentences.

You are ready to move to the next step: surveying your internal and external customers to find out what they like and dislike about your organization and its offerings.

3

Identify Your Customers' Needs—Find Out What They *Really* Want

Once you have created a quality statement or vision, you have a focal point for developing a follow-on plan of action. Although there are various opinions as to what step should come next, it is easiest and more efficient to begin by identifying customer needs. After all, the heart of any TQM effort is to do a better job of serving customers. So why not start by finding out what these people want? Most award winners agree with this idea. For example, Boise Cascade's Plan-Do-Check-Act (PDCA) Improvement Process begins, "Thoroughly understand customer's expectations and specifications" (Exhibit 3-1). The question you have to answer is: With whom should I start: internal or external customers?

There are strong reasons for starting inside. First, a TQM program needs the support of the internal personnel, and what better way to get it than by incorporating them into the process from the beginning? Second, the information gathered from these people can often be used to reduce time or increase efficiency, so you increase the chances of making changes that will pay off right away. Third, you are going to be able to gather your internal information a lot faster than the external information because most people in the organization will be cooperative. Thus, by focusing on internal customers first, you choose the path of least resistance—vital to getting a TQM program off the ground. From here, you can then move on to external customers.

There are five steps that can help you identify your customers' needs:

Exhibit 3-1. Boise Cascade's Plan-Do-Check-Act Improvement Process.

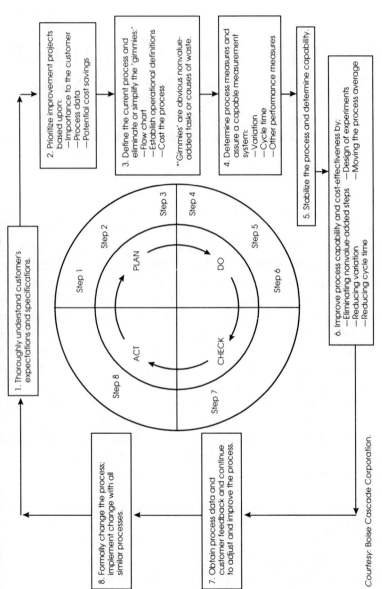

1. Thoroughly understand customer's expectations and specifications.

2. Prioritize improvement projects based upon:
   —Importance to the customer
   —Process data
   —Potential cost savings

3. Define the current process and eliminate or simplify the "gimmies:"
   —Flow chart
   —Establish operational definitions
   —Cost the process

   **"Gimmies' are obvious nonvalue-added tasks or causes of waste.

4. Determine process measures and assure a capable measurement system:
   —Variation
   —Cycle time
   —Other performance measures

5. Stabilize the process and determine capability.

6. Improve process capability and cost-effectiveness by:
   —Eliminating nonvalue-added steps
   —Reducing variation
   —Reducing cycle time
   —Design of experiments
   —Moving the process average

7. Obtain process data and customer feedback and continue to adjust and improve the process.

8. Formally change the process; implement change with all similar processes.

PLAN — DO — CHECK — ACT

Step 1, Step 2, Step 3, Step 4, Step 5, Step 6, Step 7, Step 8

Courtesy: Boise Cascade Corporation.

First   Decide the type of information you want to get from your customers—for example, whether your products are delivered on time and meet quality specifications, how responsive your associates are to external customer requests, and how satisfied your staff are with their working conditions and salaries.

Second   Become familiar with internal customer surveys that can be used to find out what your associates like and dislike about your operations and what they would like to see done differently.

Third   Become familiar with external customer surveys so that you can gather information from your customers and clients regarding what they like and dislike about your operations and what they would like to see done differently.

Fourth   Become familiar with the guidelines for designing surveys, including ways to construct effective questions and avoid responder bias, how to do a trial test of a survey, and how to distribute and collect the completed instruments.

Fifth   Create initial internal and external customer surveys, review and revise the instruments, test them, distribute the finished surveys to your customers, and collect and analyze the information.

Decide What You Want to Know

If this is your first effort at gathering information from customers, you may find this step somewhat difficult. Still, there are ways for you to decide the type of information you need.

First, identify your external customer base. You know who your associates are, but who are your outside customers? Are they a small, homogeneous group, or a diversified, heterogeneous group? When the U.S. Naval Station Mayport asked this question, it generated the following list of customers:

- Ships and sailors assigned to the station
- Aircraft squadrons and the sailors and civilians assigned to the station
- Shore commands and the personnel assigned
- Retired personnel who use the facilities
- Dependent spouses and children of the station's military personnel
- Higher authority (those to whom the naval station reports)
- Guests of the naval station
- The state of Florida
- U.S. taxpayers

Your customer base may not be as extensive, but you should write down as comprehensive a list of customers as you can generate. To get started, ask yourself this question: Whom do I serve? After you have written down as many different groups as you can think of, show the list to some of your key associates and ask them to add any you have left off.

Your list may be redundant; that is, people who fit into one of the categories may also fit into others. For example, in the list from Mayport, naval personnel are also U.S. taxpayers. The important thing is to be comprehensive and not worry about selectivity or double counting.

Now you have to answer two questions: What do these different customer groups want? How can I satisfy them? To guide you, let's look at another example: Valley Hospital Medical Center, another award-winning organization, and one of its primary customer groups, patients. What does the medical center have to do to satisfy the needs of these individuals? The obvious answer is to provide effective health care. But what does this mean? What specifically does the medical center have to do? And what does all of this mean to the customer (patients)? Here are five answers, along with what each means:

Objective	What This Means to the Customer
Have efficient admission procedures	Get the patient checked into the facility as quickly as possible
Offer the best medical care possible	Have the requisite doctors, nurses, and equipment to provide for the patient's needs

Keep the patient apprised of his or her diagnosis and treatment	Tell the person what is going on and answer any questions the individual may have
Provide nourishing, healthy food	Feed the patient food that is properly cooked and tastes good
Maintain an accurate accounting of all financial charges	Be sure that the bill is accurate and fair

By reviewing the above information, a hospital administrator can develop questions to be asked of patients in order to evaluate how satisfied they are with the health care services they received. Here are five questions that reflect information related to the above areas:

1. How long did it take for you to be admitted to the hospital? _____ minutes

2. How would you rate the quality of medical service that you received from our staff?

   1   2   3   4   5   6   7   8   9   10
   Poor   Excellent

3. Were all of your medical questions answered to your satisfaction?   Yes   No (please explain)

   _____

   _____

4. How would you rate the overall quality of the food?

   1   2   3   4   5   6   7   8   9   10
   Poor   Excellent

5. Overall, how would you rate the hospital's billing procedures?

   1   2   3   4   5   6   7   8   9   10
   Poor   Excellent

These examples of the types of questions that might appear on the survey help illustrate how to link your survey questions to the information you need to know.

Another, and supplemental, approach to surveys is the identification of key indicator categories such as safety and quality, which can be measured through internal operations. These indicators help the organization identify the work that it has to do well if it wants to remain a quality-driven organization. Exhibit 3-2 provides a good example: Wainwright Industries' indicators and frequency measurements. This information is an important supplement to what can be learned by surveying customers. Notice in the exhibit, for example, that internal customer satisfaction is measured, among other things, by attendance and turnover. The company believes that if people come to work on time and worker

Exhibit 3-2. Key strategic indicator categories at Wainwright Industries.

Key Indicator Category	Key Quality Indicator	Measurement Frequency
Safety	Recordable accidents	Daily
	Facilities index	Daily
	Waste stream	Monthly
	Safety improvements	Weekly
Internal Customer Satisfaction	Index rating	Weekly
	Total plant improvements	Weekly
	Attendance	Weekly
	Appraisal timeliness	Weekly
	Associate turnover	Weekly
External Customer Satisfaction	Index rating	Weekly
	Customer complaints	Weekly
	External parts per million ratings	Weekly/monthly
	Delivery time	Weekly
	Supplier delivery time	Weekly
6 Sigma Quality[a]	Internal parts per million ratings	Weekly/monthly
	Quality costs	Monthly
	Supplier quality	Weekly
	Pareto analyais top-10 problems	Monthly

Business Performance (operational)	Tonnage	Daily
	Value-added	Daily
	Set-up cycle time	Weekly
	Uptime	Weekly
	Product cycle time	Weekly
	Overtime	Weekly
	Inventory turn	Monthly
	Reactionary maintenance	Weekly
Business Performance (support services)	Quote timeliness	Weekly
	Financial statements	Monthly
	Requisition cycle time	Weekly
	Accounts Receivable over 90 days	Weekly
	Lost calls	Weekly
	Invoicing accuracy	Weekly
	401(k) participation	Quarterly
	Promotion percentage	Monthly
	Accounts payable calls	Weekly
	Meeting efficiency	Weekly

[a]3.4 errors per 1 million parts.
Courtesy: Wainwright Industries.

turnover is low, the employees think the company is a good place to work. Similarly, external customer satisfaction can be measured, among other ways, by complaints and delivery time. If the number of complaints is low and products are delivered as promised, the customer will be satisfied. A close look at the key indicator categories in the exhibit shows that there are a host of ways of measuring quality. Remember, however, these are not a substitute for a survey; they are a supplement to them.

Still another way of understanding customer needs is to ask yourself: What will this individual want in the future? The answers help you prepare a long-range, customer-focused strategy. Before you begin trying to forecast needs five years down the road, however, it is often necessary to find out what the customer wants today and in the near future. You may be able to do this exercise based on what you already know about your customers, as Zytec has done. Exhibit 3-3 shows some of the needs of Zytec's customers in 1994 and those predicted for the year 2000. This strategy is fundamental to the company's efforts to improve customer service, and it helps explain why Zytec is considered one of the best power supply companies in the world.

By asking yourself about future customer needs, you can often generate questions that help identify or elaborate on products or

Exhibit 3-3. Power supply product customer needs, 1994–2000.

Customer Needs	1994 Typical	2000 Typical
Improved quality	400–2,000 ppm[a]	3.4 ppm[a]
Accelerated time to market for prototype	7–16 weeks	5–10 weeks
Increased efficiency/ reduction in heat	70–75% efficient	75–90% efficient
Lower price	$0.35–$1.00/watt	$0.20–$0.40/watt
Reduced output noise	2%	1%
Reduced operating voltages	3.3–5 volts	1.5–5 volts
Power supply intelligence	Limited intelligence	Integrated intelligence
Distributed power	Limited application	Increased application
Quality	> 4 sigma	> 6 sigma
Delivery frequency	Weekly	Daily
Repair on-time delivery	85%	97%
Repair cycle time	12 days	5 days
Product warranty	1–2 years	Lifetime
Product replacement	10–15 days	1-day exchange
Product locations	United States and Europe	Worldwide
Time to build first prototype	7–16 weeks	5–10 weeks
Time to build initial product	20–32 weeks	12–16 weeks
Geographic servicing	United States and Europe	North America, Europe, and Far East

[a]Parts per million.
Source: Zytec Corporation.

services your customer would like you to supply in the future. Then, based on your conclusions, you can write survey questions.

Become Familiar With Internal Customer Surveys

You can get feedback from your internal customers regarding what they like and dislike about your operations in a number of ways. For example, you could interview associates and ask them to provide you with direct, frank comments. However, most employees will not give much negative information, so this approach is bound to provide you, at best, with only some of the things you need to know about the attitudes and feelings of your internal customers. A simpler, and more effective, way is to follow the approach of quality award winners and use a formal employee survey that asks specific questions and then gives the respondents a chance to make additional comments. Exhibits 3-4 and 3-5 provide select examples. Read these before continuing.

Notice the following salient characteristics of the two questionnaires:

- They are fairly short; they can be completed within 30 minutes.
- They direct the respondent by offering alternative answers (*excellent, good, fair, poor*) as well as the opportunity to provide individual written responses.
- There is anonymity. No one needs to know who filled out the questionnaire.
- The responses provide a basis for conducting an analysis and drawing conclusions.

By keeping these data on hand and using them as a benchmark, you can compare responses from future surveys and see where you are doing better or more poorly.

(text continues on page 52)

Exhibit 3-4. Wild Oats staff survey.

This survey has been created so that you can anonymously relate your experiences as a staff member of Wild Oats. We will be using the numerical portion to come up with a store "Happiness Index," which will tell us if morale is giddy or suicidal. This feedback will help us create a better working environment for everyone. Please do your best to complete this survey in an honest and open manner and with as much detail and explanation as possible.

Please rate your responses by circling the number that most closely describes your experience. Feel free to use the back of these sheets for additional comments.

1. *How happy are you with your job overall?*
   Not happy at all .... Ecstatic
   1   2   3   4   5   6   7   8   9   10
   Any comments or suggestions?

2. *How do you feel about your benefits at Wild Oats?*
   Terrible .... Great
   1   2   3   4   5   6   7   8   9   10
   Any comments or suggestions?

3. *How do you feel about the pay levels at Wild Oats as compared to similar employers?*
   Worse than most .... Ecstatic
   1   2   3   4   5   6   7   8   9   10
   Any comments or suggestions?

4. *How do you feel about the employee review system at Wild Oats?*
   Hate it .... Love it
   1   2   3   4   5   6   7   8   9   10
   Any comments or suggestions?

5. *How is the overall morale in your store?*
   Awful .... Wonderful

   | 1 | 2 | 3 | 4 | 5 | 6 | 7 | 8 | 9 | 10 |

   Any comments or suggestions?

6. *How do you feel about the responsibilities of your job?*
   Too little .... Too much

   | 1 | 2 | 3 | 4 | 5 | 6 | 7 | 8 | 9 | 10 |

   Any comments or suggestions?

7. *How effectively is your store managed?*
   Very poorly .... Very well

   | 1 | 2 | 3 | 4 | 5 | 6 | 7 | 8 | 9 | 10 |

   Any comments or suggestions?

8. *How effective is your department manager?*
   Remarkably bad .... Terrific

   | 1 | 2 | 3 | 4 | 5 | 6 | 7 | 8 | 9 | 10 |

   Any comments or suggestions?

9. *Why do you come to work every day?*
   Have to .... Want to

   | 1 | 2 | 3 | 4 | 5 | 6 | 7 | 8 | 9 | 10 |

   Any comments or suggestions?

10. *How does Wild Oats compare to your previous employers?*
    Worse .... Same .... Much better

    | 1 | 2 | 3 | 4 | 5 | 6 | 7 | 8 | 9 | 10 |

    Any comments or suggestions?

(continues)

Exhibit 3-4. *(Continued)*

11. What department do you work in? (optional) _____

12. How long have you worked for Wild Oats? _____

13. How do you feel about the training and orientation program you experienced when you started? Do you feel you understand the procedures, policies, and responsibilities that are part of your job? How would you change things?

14. What do you like *least* about your job and/or the company? Please explain.

15. What do you like *most* about your job and/or the company? Please explain.

16. What would you change if you were the owner?

Source: Wild Oats.

Become Familiar With External Customer Surveys

Follow a similar strategy in surveying your external customers. This survey instrument, however, has to be more meticulously prepared than the internal one because it must attract the customer's attention and encourage the individual to complete and return it. The survey has to be well designed and well laid out, easy to complete, and contain questions that the customer considers appropriate. Like the employee questionnaire, it also must be brief, allow for anonymity, and provide information that can be quantified and analyzed. Exhibits 3-6 and 3-7 are examples; they are similar to the employee surveys.

One of the award-winning companies I studied surveyed its

(text continues on page 58)

Exhibit 3-5. Henry Lee attitude survey.

Please carefully read each of the following statements and circle the choice that most accurately reflects your opinion. Do not spend a lot of time thinking about your answers, since these questions are designed only to determine your feelings and attitudes.

1. How satisfied are you with the supervision you receive?
   a. Extremely satisfied
   b. Well satisfied
   c. Moderately satisfied
   d. Somewhat dissatisfied
   e. Very dissatisfied
2. Which of the following best describes the effect of the supervision you receive?
   a. It influences me to give a lot of extra effort to my work.
   b. It influences me to give some extra effort to my work.
   c. It does not affect the amount of extra effort I exert.
   d. It influences me to give somewhat less effort than I would ordinarily give.
   e. It influences me to give much less effort than I would ordinarily give.
3. How much confidence and trust does your supervisor have in you?
   a. Total
   b. A great deal
   c. Some
   d. A little
   e. None
4. How supportive is your supervisor in helping you out when you have a problem?
   a. Totally supportive
   b. Very supportive
   c. Somewhat supportive
   d. A little supportive
   e. Not supportive at all
5. How free do you feel to discuss important matters with your supervisor?
   a. Totally free
   b. Very free
   c. Somewhat free
   d. Not very free
   e. Not free at all
6. How often does your supervisor try to get your ideas and opinions when solving job-related problems?
   a. Always
   b. Usually
   c. Occasionally
   d. Seldom
   e. Never

(continues)

Exhibit 3-5. *(Continued)*

7. To what extent does your supervisor know and understand the problems you face in getting your work done?
   a. Fully knows and understands them
   b. Pretty much knows and understands them
   c. Has a fairly good idea of what they are
   d. Does not really know and understand them
   e. Has no idea of what is going on

8. Are you treated fairly by your supervisor?
   a. Always
   b. Usually
   c. Occasionally
   d. Seldom
   e. Never

9. How would you describe communication between you and your supervisor?
   a. Always open and candid
   b. Usually open and candid
   c. More open and candid than closed
   d. Somewhat closed and guarded
   e. Always closed and guarded

10. What are your feelings about the work you do?
   a. I really like it.
   b. I like it.
   c. I'm indifferent about it.
   d. I don't like it.
   e. I dislike it.

11. When you finish a day's work, do you feel that you've accomplished something worthwhile?
   a. All the time
   b. Most of the time
   c. More often than not
   d. Less than half the time
   e. Never or almost never

12. How do you feel about your work load?
   a. It's almost always too heavy.
   b. It's often too heavy.
   c. It's sometimes too heavy.
   d. It's seldom too heavy.
   e. It's never too heavy.

13. How much cooperation and teamwork is there in your department?
   a. A very great deal
   b. A fairly high amount
   c. A moderate amount
   d. Not very much at all
   e. None

14. How much cooperation and teamwork is there between your department and other departments with which you must coordinate or interact?
   a. A very great deal
   b. A fairly high amount
   c. A moderate amount
   d. Not very much at all
   e. None

15. How much authority do you have to make decisions?
    a. I can make any decisions that are necessary to getting my job done.
    b. I can make most of the decisions that are necessary to getting my job done.
    c. I can make a fair number of the decisions that are necessary to getting my job done.
    d. I cannot make many decisions on my own; I have to check with my supervisor.
    e. I cannot make any decision on my own; I have to check everything with my supervisor.

16. Are you afraid of making a mistake on your job because of the trouble you might get into?
    a. Never
    b. Almost never
    c. Seldom
    d. Occasionally
    e. Always

17. What is your view of morale in your department?
    a. Excellent
    b. Good
    c. Average
    d. Poor
    e. Terrible

18. What is your view of morale in the company at large?
    a. Excellent
    b. Good
    c. Average
    d. Poor
    e. Terrible

19. Do you get credit when you do a good job?
    a. Always
    b. Almost always
    c. Usually
    d. Seldom
    e. Never

20. How would you rate the job-related training you have received?
    a. Excellent
    b. Good
    c. Fair
    d. Poor
    e. Terrible

21. How well does the company provide you with the machinery and equipment needed to get your job done?
    a. Extremely well
    b. Very well
    c. Well
    d. Not very well
    e. Poorly

22. How much attention does the company show for the overall welfare of all employees?
    a. A great deal
    b. A fair amount
    c. Some
    d. Little
    e. Just about none

(continues)

Exhibit 3-5. *(Continued)*

23. How would you rate Henry Lee as a place to work when compared with other companies where you have worked?
    a. Excellent
    b. Good
    c. Average
    d. Poor
    e. Terrible

24. How long have you worked for Henry Lee?
    a. Less than 1 year
    b. 1–3 years
    c. 4–7 years
    d. 8–10 years
    e. More than 10 years

25. What are the two things that you like best about working for the company?

    1. _____
       _____

    2. _____
       _____

26. What are the two things that you like least about working for the company?

    1. _____
       _____

    2. _____
       _____

27. If you could change two things in the company, what would they be?

    1. _____
       _____

    2. _____
       _____

Thank you for your assistance.

Source: The Henry Lee Company.

Exhibit 3-6. Phelps County Bank external customer survey.

OUR COMMITMENT TO SERVICE EXCELLENCE CREED

We, the employee owners of Phelps County Bank, in order to form a more perfect service record, endeavor to maintain high standards, ensure customer satisfaction, promote the general principles of courtesy, and secure our commitment to the customers; do ordain and establish this dedication for the customers of Phelps County Bank.

We shall make every customer our number one priority; shall be committed to a quality of service that exceeds expectations; and shall treat each customer as an individual in a kind, courteous and respectful manner.

SERVICE ASSURANCE

Check all of the types of service you use at PCB:

__ checking   __ saving   __ certificate of
__ loans   __ lockbox   deposit
                                 __ direct deposit

Check the location you use most frequently:

__ Rolla-downtown   __ Rolla-campus   __ Rolla-drive-in
__ St. James   (Hwy 72)

When do you normally do your banking?

Day of week _____   Time of day _____

Would you say that the waiting time, if any, at the bank is acceptable?   __ Yes   __ No

If you have had a problem with any of your banking services and have called or visited the bank to discuss it, please check one choice from *each* column below.

__ Response time was very fast   __ Results were more than
__ Response time was   expected
   acceptable   __ Results were acceptable
__ Response time was slow   __ Results were not acceptable

Do the employee-owners seem to make an effort to know your name?

__ Yes   __ No

(continues)

Exhibit 3-6. *(Continued)*

How would you rate the konwledge of PCB owners with whom you have had contact:

— Excellent
— Average
— Below average

Will you open other accounts at PCB as the need arises?

— Yes   — No

Are there any other services you would like to see the bank offer?

_____

_____

_____

Would you like to join our customer service advisory team?

— Yes. *Please be sure to write your name and phone number below!*
— No

OPTIONAL: If you feel comfortable, please write your name and phone number below.

Name: _____   Phone number _____

COMMENTS _____

_____

_____

Courtesy: Phelps County Bank.

external customers to find out how service could be improved. Some of the demographic data that were collected included buying habits and suggestions for improved service. The greatest number of suggestions (19 percent of all responses) were for extended shopping hours. However, a statistical analysis revealed that occasional shoppers who purchased minimal amounts of goods were more likely than any other group to want the stores to stay open later. Customers who purchased the greatest amount of merchandise wanted more associate assistance and shorter waiting lines.

(text continues on page 62)

Exhibit 3-7. First Union external customer survey.

1. Which First Union branch were you banking with today? (Please print name of branch.)

_____

2. What was the purpose of your visit today?
   (Check all that apply).
   1. Make a teller transaction, such as deposit or withdrawal ☐
   2. Discuss a loan ☐
   3. Open a new account ☐
   4. Close an account ☐
   5. Talk with the Branch Manager or Customer Sales/Service Personnel ☐
   6. Solve a problem ☐
   7. Other _____

3. How would you rate the following in terms of TODAY's visit to First Union?

	Excellent 4	Good 3	Fair 2	Poor 1
1. Speed of service	___	___	___	___
2. Courtesy or friendliness of our staff	___	___	___	___
3. Knowledge of our staff	___	___	___	___
4. Concern for you and your banking needs	___	___	___	___
5. Availability of appropriate banking personnel	___	___	___	___
6. Wait in teller line	___	___	___	___
7. Convenience of branch locations	___	___	___	___

4. How often do you bank with a First Union branch?
   1. Less than 1 time a week ☐
   2. 1–2 times a week ☐
   3. 3 or more times a week ☐

(continues)

Exhibit 3-7. *(Continued)*

5. How long have you been banking with First Union?
   1. Less than six months ☐
   2. Six months to less than 2 years ☐
   3. 2 years to less than 5 years ☐
   4. 5 years and longer ☐

6. How often do you currently use a First Union 24 Hour Banking machine?
   1. Do not currently use ☐
   2. Less than 1 time a month ☐
   3. 2–4 times a month ☐
   4. More than 1 time a week ☐

7. If you have used a First Union 24 Hour Banking machine, please answer the following questions.

	Very 3	Somewhat 2	Not At All 1
1. Was it dependable?	____	____	____
2. Was the location convenient?	____	____	____
3. Was the area around the machine clean?	____	____	____
4. Was it easy to use?	____	____	____
5. Were you satisfied with the speed of the machine?	____	____	____
6. Was the area well lighted?	____	____	____

8. Based on your OVERALL experience with First Union, how would you rate each of the following?

	Excellent 4	Good 3	Fair 2	Poor 1
1. Providing error-free banking services	____	____	____	____
2. Providing speedy service	____	____	____	____
3. Making suggestions so I can more easily make decisions about banking products	____	____	____	____
4. Providing personalized service	____	____	____	____

5. Being friendly and courteous   _____ _____ _____ _____

6. Getting requests or problems resolved quickly and efficiently   _____ _____ _____ _____

9. Do the personnel in the First Union branch you most often use make you feel valued for your business?

     ☐ Yes   ☐ No

10. Has any member of our staff been especially helpful?

     ☐ Yes   ☐ No

If yes, please let us know so we can show our appreciation to this person. _____

11. Please share with us what you consider to be the most important thing First Union can do to provide better-quality service.

_____

_____

_____

_____

_____

Thank you for taking time to complete our comment card. With your help we will continue to work toward the highest-quality customer service possible.

If you would like for us to respond, please print your name and address below.

Name   Mr./Mrs./Ms. _____

Address _____

City _____ State _____ Zip _____

You may telephone me at:

(home) _____

(work) _____

Courtesy: First Union National Bank of Dade/Monroe Counties Florida.

As a result of careful analysis, the company was able to address the needs of its most important buyers—something that would not have been done had the company simply added up the number of customer suggestions and addressed the one that appeared most frequently.

Know the Guidelines for Designing Surveys

Now that you have had a chance to examine examples of internal and external survey instruments and have reviewed some of the types of feedback you are seeking, let's pinpoint the basic rules that need to be followed in designing these data collection forms:

• Keep the survey short and to the point. An external survey should be three pages at most and not ask more than twenty questions. An internal survey should be no longer than four pages and ask no more than thirty questions.

• All questions should be easy to answer. If it takes more than 30 minutes to complete a written survey, reduce the number of questions or make them simpler. If a question has more than one major idea, try breaking it into two or more questions. Consider the following:

> How long have you worked for the company, and what do you do?

The problem with this question is that the individual may have worked for the company for ten years and had three different jobs. If you want to know the individual's current job or position, rewrite the question in this way:

> How long have you worked for the company?
>
> What is your current position?

• Unless it will bias the survey, give respondents some choices in question answers. Let's say you want to know how long the individual has worked for the company. Perhaps you believe that those who are new to your organization (less than one year) have a different point of view regarding working conditions and salaries from those who have been with the company for longer periods of time. In this case, your question could be stated this way:

How long have you worked for the company?
_____ less than 1 year   _____ 1–5 years
_____ more than 5 years

This approach also helps you categorize the information and conduct comparative analysis. For example, you can now compare length of service with response to how satisfied the personnel are with working conditions and salaries. This is a good example of how a well-designed question can make it easier to group the respondents and draw conclusions.

• Be sure that the respondents are willing and able to answer the question. Stay away from controversial or threatening topics such as: "Do you think we have too many people working in the company?" Also, do not ask people to sign their names to the form, and refrain from putting any markings on the form that would lead them to believe you can identify them.

• Be careful not to bias the responses by offering suggestions or information that is likely to influence the respondents. For example, do not ask employees if they feel they are underpaid, paid fairly, or overpaid. Most people will respond that they are underpaid or paid fairly; no one is going to say he or she is overpaid. Similarly, do not ask customers how they feel about the personnel by giving them extreme positions such as:

Which of the following best describes your feelings about the service that is provided by the company?

_____ The service is good, and I think the personnel try hard to make it even better.
_____ The service is extremely poor, and I don't think the personnel care one way or the other.

Given these alternatives, most customers are going to be complimentary about the service. A better approach is to offer a continuum for customers. Here is an example:

> How would you describe the service that is provided by the company?
>
> 1   2   3   4   5   6   7   8   9   10
> Extremely   Average   Excellent
> poor

• Do not ask questions that people cannnot answer; all you will get, at best, is an educated guess. Consider this question:

> How do our hospital's prices compare to those of similar-sized hospitals around the country where you have received medical treatment?
>
> 1   2   3   4   5   6   7   8   9   10
> Much   About   Lower
> higher   the
>   same

The question assumes that the individual has had medical treatment at other hospitals around the country and is able to compare the prices.

• Avoid putting the respondent on the spot by asking the individual to say something negative about a competitor or fellow worker. For example, if the hospital in the previous question wanted to compare itself to other local hospitals, it should not ask the respondent, "Of the following hospitals, which one offers the best customer service and which offers the poorest?" Instead, the hospital should ask the respondent to rank-order the group of choices without using the words *best* and *poorest*. Here is an example:

> How would you rank the overall customer service of each of the following? Place 1 next to your first choice, a 2 next to your second choice, etc.

_____ Hospital A
_____ Hospital B
_____ Hospital C
_____ Hospital D

• Group the objective questions based on answer format. For example, if your first question asks the individual to place a check mark next to the preferred answer, group all of the check mark questions in the front of the questionnaire. Do not switch to a ranking format (such as the one above) and then go to some form of fill-in question, and then return to a check mark question. Changing answer formats is confusing to the person filling out the survey.

• As best you can, group similar questions. For example, if you have four questions related to customer waiting time, present them one after the other. A logical organization makes it easier for the respondent to fill out the survey.

• Put the simplest questions at the beginning of the survey, and save the more difficult ones for later. Chances are that the individual will complete the instrument because most people continue filling out a survey if they are almost finished, but they will throw it away if they find themselves being confused or stumped early on. So make it easy for them to get started.

• Test the survey with a small group before you approve it for distribution at large. This strategy helps significantly reduce the chances of mistakes, inconsistencies, or vaguely stated instructions or questions. Ask these early respondents to make any suggested changes they would like, including rewriting or rephrasing questions or simply writing "unclear" or "What does this mean?" next to anything they have trouble understanding.

• Make all of the necessary changes, and have another copy of the instrument drawn up. Now check it for length and style, and ensure that there are no additional mistakes or problems. Once you are satisfied with the results, make copies, and begin distributing them.

• Decide how to collect the surveys and who will see them. Those from internal customers should be completed and placed in a box or other container that is sealed and opened only by you or your representative. If employees are concerned that their comments will be traced back to them, hire an outsider, such as a university professor, and pay the individual a fee to analyze and record all of the information, but not return the questionnaires to you. If your company is quite small, confidentiality will not be necessary; most associates will assume that their answers are not confidential, and they have probably already told you a lot of what is in their survey. In either event, however, be sure that all of your internal customers feel comfortable that the information will not be used against them.

In the case of external customers, if they fill the surveys out in your store or company, provide a container or box where they can be deposited. You need to think about how you are going to get back the surveys from those who take them away from the store or, if you include them with the monthly bill, receive them by mail. If they take the survey with them, supply a return envelope so the material can be mailed back. If your budget allows, design a one-page survey that can be folded up and becomes a self-addressed return envelope that needs merely to be dropped in the mail.

• Record the information, and take a look at the initial conclusions. Do the answers provide you the type of feedback you were seeking? If you designed the survey correctly, the answer should be yes. Nevertheless, you may realize that there are other questions you should have asked but did not. Unless this is a major problem (and it should not be), this is a learning error that you can correct when you revise the survey for future use. For example, if you intend to poll your customers twice a year, note the changes that you will want to include in the future version. If you intend to survey customers on an ongoing basis, make the revision in the next printing of the survey. If the data are carefully analyzed, you will obtain some interesting and meaningful findings.

Create Your Own Survey Instruments

It will take some time for you to create internal and external survey instruments and test them. The following worksheet will be helpful in designing a survey. Look over the five questions in it (and make copies of the worksheet for those who will be helping in this effort). Then begin writing down your initial ideas associated with each answer. You can flesh them out later. The important thing is to get started now. Finally, set yourself a goal: to have an internal and an external survey completed and ready to be tested within 30 days. Then, based on the information received, you can begin organizing your total quality effort.

Designing Our Own Surveys

1. What are the most important things we have to do to succeed in our business? (Write down these key factors for success, and, where possible, indicate how you would know if you were doing them. For example, if you say, "Keep customers satisified," how would you know if this were being done? What are some of the forms of feedback that would allow you to evaluate your success in this area?)

2. Who are our internal customers, and what would we like to know from them that would help us improve the quality of our operations?

3. Based on the above information, what are ten questions we would like to ask internal customers?

4. Who are our external customers, and what would we like to know from them that would help us improve the quality of our operations?

5. Based on the above information, what are ten questions we would like to ask our external customers?

Combine your answers to the worksheet questions with those from colleagues who are assisting you, and put together the two surveys. Be sure to use the guidelines that were suggested in this chapter. Then test the instruments, make the necessary changes, and begin collecting the information. Based on this information, you can begin organizing your total quality effort.

4

Design the Organization Structure—Simply and Cost-Effectively

Once you have gathered information from your internal and external customers, you have an idea of the types of quality problems you would like to deal with and perhaps some of the steps you would like to implement. However, unless you are going to do all of this by yourself, an effective TQM organization structure is needed. This process is not as difficult as it might appear. But remember that your initial efforts are likely to need revision and modification, so these first efforts are often just the beginning of an organizing process that will require ongoing tweaking.

There are four steps that can help you design a simple, cost-effective structure:

First   Decide who will head the TQM effort. One individual or group should be responsible for overseeing the effort.

Second   Look at some of the organizing options that can be of value, among them, the use of quality councils, quality teams, team leaders, and facilitators.

Third   Examine some of the approaches used by award-winning companies, note some of the ways in which they employ simple, efficient organizing techniques to focus and direct their TQM efforts, and choose those that can be of most practical value to your organization.

Fourth   Use the information you have gathered to create an initial TQM structure. After you have tried it out, be prepared to modify this organizational arrangement in order to meet the specific needs of your enterprise.

Decide Who Will Head the Effort

No matter how your TQM effort is organized, appoint one individual or a group to assume responsibility for the success of the program. When there is no leader, the overall quality effort typically fails; although everyone may be collectively responsible for improving quality, no one is personally responsible. Moreover, one of the biggest complaints of many associates is that they do not have the time to do their job and work on quality-related issues. They fail to realize (or refuse to acknowledge) that quality *is* their job. So some top-down leadership is needed.

If your enterprise is small and requires little formal organization in order to pursue a quality program, consider heading the effort yourself or assigning it to a specific individual. In the latter case, however, you cannot just appoint the person. You have to give the individual some work release time, so the person can help design quality programs, measure and evaluate feedback, report back to you regarding progress, and discuss future developments. If the job is too large for one person, consider using a TQM committee. To help you decide which approach is better, explore some of the key organizing options that can be of value.

Look at Some of Your Organizing Options

You have a number of options or alternative approaches from which to choose in organizing the TQM effort. Before creating a structure, be sure you understand the role and functions of some key TQM groups.

Identify TQM Groups and Roles

Among the different types of committees that are often used to promote TQM efforts, the most common are quality councils, quality teams, and leaders and facilitators.

Quality Control

Because the job is too big for one person, virtually very successful TQM-driven company has a committee that directs the overall effort. This committee is often known as the quality council, although it is commonly referred to as "the council" or "QC" for short. The group typically reports directly to the president, who, along with at least a couple of other senior-level managers, serve as members. In addition, it is common to find representation from around the company. Broad representation can be a very effective organizing strategy because the QC is responsible for deciding which TQM efforts to fund. By having council members who understand the specific workings of each department, it is possible to identify the TQM projects that are most feasible or will provide the organization the greatest increase in quality for the time and money that are expended. Quite often these projects are a result of suggestions from associates who feel that the organization can save money or increase quality by investigating a particular problem or implementing a specific strategy. In some enterprises, the QC responds to all suggestions. A QC that has people on it who are knowledgeable about the organization's operations, and may even work in the same area as the person submitting the suggestion, is in a good position to explain its decision on each suggestion.

If you decide that a QC is a good idea (and we will be exploring the roles and responsibilities of this group a little later in the chapter), keep in mind that the committee should not be too large. In a company with twenty-five or fewer employees, a QC of just five members is often adequate to get the job done. After all, in a small operation, there are likely to be a number of employees who understand just about all facets of the company. In a firm of twenty-six to one hundred, a QC of seven people is usually sufficient. In an enterprise of more than one hundred people, a group of ten to twelve is usually needed.

Whatever number you choose, be careful not to make the group too large. The QC is responsible for deciding how the entire TQM strategy will be implemented, and the bigger the committee is, the longer it will take to arrive at decisions. Additionally, the QC has to meet periodically to plan and implement total quality–related decisions, so you will need to set aside a particular time for meeting. The more people there are on the committee, the more difficult it becomes to get full attendance and the greater the problems are associated with pulling people off the job to attend a meeting. So in choosing the committee size, try to keep it on the low side.

Quality Teams

Total quality is a group effort. In order to get everyone in your company actively involved in this effort, it is important to give each person an opportunity to be a quality team member. At any point in time, not everyone may be on a team; however, eventually everyone should have an opportunity to participate. In the initial TQM efforts, it is a good idea to have only one or two teams and for the QC to assign them simple objectives. In this way, the groups can quickly finish their tasks and report their successes. These good results help build momentum among the other associates to become members of a quality team.

Quality teams go by a number of names. Some organizations refer to them as PIT teams. (PIT stands for "process improvement team".) Others do not like the negative connotation of the acronym PIT; they prefer "Q team" with the Q standing for "quality." And this is the way they will be referred to throughout this book.

The QC is typically responsible for assigning people to Q teams, and the projects to which the teams are assigned are usually determined in one of two ways:

1. The QC members see a quality-related problem that needs to be solved. They put together a team to investigate this problem and report back with suggestions or recommendations.
2. Associates submit suggestions to the QC, which forms a Q team to look into the matter.

A Q team can be made up of members of one department only or individuals from two or more departments. If the problem under investigation is confined to a particular department, commonly the Q team members come from that department. For example, the team members of a group studying how to reduce the time needed to load delivery trucks most likely will all come from the warehouse. Conversely, if the problem cuts across departmental lines, commonly the team members will come from departments that are most affected. For example, a team studying how to reduce the time needed to fill customer orders would likely have members from the sales department, information systems (computer) department, warehouse, and delivery, among others. After the team members are determined, the group will meet and begin its work.

All Q teams use fairly similar procedures. Here is a brief description of the life of one of the teams I followed during my investigation.

1. A specific weekly time was set for the meetings: 10 A.M. every Monday.

2. The first meeting was used to define the problem to be studied: How to reduce the time for loading trucks in the warehouse from the current 29 minutes down to 24 minutes.

3. Each individual was assigned a specific task related to the problem: examining (a) how the warehouse received the computerized list of what was to be loaded on each truck, (b) the procedures used to pick the products from the warehouse shelves, and (c) the methods used to load the trucks. One person was also assigned to keep minutes of the meeting, which were then typed and distributed to the Q team members, as well as to the QC.

4. During the next three meetings, each member reported what he or she had learned and identified additional information that was needed and/or steps that had to be implemented in reducing time. For example, one member suggested reracking the merchandise, so that faster-moving items were located closer to the trucks and could be loaded more quickly. A second suggested creating a more detailed computer printout so that the pickers could more easily identify the merchandise to be taken off the shelves for loading. A third recommended that each computer

printout be available 15 minutes before the picking began, to avoid delay in letting the associates know what they were to load so they would be ready to begin the moment their shift started.

5. Based on these suggestions, Q team members were given follow-up assignments related to the cost and feasibility of the recommendations. They began gathering information to answer questions such as: How much will it cost to rerack the merchandise? How much time will this save? Is it worth the investment? If so, how should this recommendation be implemented?

6. At the weekly meetings, members continued to report progress, share their data, and discuss ideas. As the project started coming to fruition, they directed their attention to formalizing the findings and putting them into a final report. Each member wrote his or her part of the report, and then one person rewrote the overall final report, which had five sections: (a) statement of the problem, (b) analysis of the information, (c) recommendations for action, (d) a cost-benefit analysis showing why the recommendations were beneficial, and (e) an implementation plan showing how the recommendations could be put into action.

7. The report was submitted to the QC to review the nature and scope of the project.

8. The Q team then presented the report to the QC in a 30-minute session, followed by another 30 minutes of questions and answers. The QC approved the Q team's recommendations regarding reracking the merchandise and redesigning the computer printout.

After the team has completed its task and made its recommendations to the QC, it is up to the QC to decide whether to accept, modify, or ignore the information. In some cases the recommendation is easy to implement, costs very little, and can quickly increase quality, so the QC votes to enact the recommendation. In other cases, the team members all come from the same department, and there is money in this unit's budget to pay for the implementation, so the QC agrees to let the department make the recommended changes. If the council decides not to go forward with the Q team's recommendation, it is common to write a memo explaining why. If nothing else, the explanation prevents the team from feeling that the council did not appreciate all of the time and effort it spent investigating the problem and formulating the recommendations.

Leaders and Facilitators

Q teams, the heart of most quality efforts, typically start out by writing either a mission statement or an objective that will guide their efforts. In small businesses, it is usually sufficient simply to write down the purpose of the group—for example:

> Reduce the time needed to load delivery trucks from 29 minutes to 24 minutes.

> Increase the number of customer applications being processed from 10 an hour to 14.

> Analyze the current parking situation and determine how to eliminate the need for parking on the lawns.

A statement of this sort helps provide a focal point for the group's action.

Now, as it pursues the objective, it will need a group leader. Sometimes the group makes this decision, but usually the QC or the department manager assumes this responsibility. There are seven criteria or benchmarks that are used in deciding who will be a good Q team leader. Quite often these can be described by the acronym C-H-A-N-G-E-R, a word that also reflects the primary purpose of the team:

C-H-A-N-G-E-R

1. *Communicative.* The individual must be willing and able to elicit and share information.
2. *High achieving.* The leader must want the team to succeed and be prepared to play a major role in this process.
3. *Analytical.* The leader must be able to sift through data and be able to draw conclusions that are not obvious to the average team member.
4. *Negotiative.* The individual must be able to work well with team members, the QC, and associates in other depart-

ments so as to generate support for the team's efforts and create a win-win environment.

5. _Generalist._ The leader must be able to see everyone's point of view and not become bogged down in detail.
6. _Experienced._ The individual must have been in a leadership position before, so he or she understands the fundamentals of managing people effectively.
7. _Results oriented._ The leader must be guided by the cost-benefit payoff for the company and not some personal gain.

At the time the Q team leader is chosen, a facilitator is appointed for the group. This person, who is _not_ a formal member of the team, is responsible for attending meetings, keeping things moving smoothly, and ensuring that the group continues to focus on the quality issue and not get sidetracked. If there are a large number of Q teams in the organization, a facilitator may work with two or three of them.

Leaders and facilitators usually need some form of group training. Small organizations, with fewer than fifty employees, can accomplish this with a meeting that focuses on the activities and responsibilities of both individuals—leaders and facilitators. The goal of this meeting is to ensure that people understand what is expected of them and review some of the specific behaviors they should employ in carrying out these tasks. Larger organizations may conduct a formal training program (often lasting from 4 hours to a full day) that reviews the basics of group leadership and facilitation and provides the participants with a list of dos and don'ts that can help guide their efforts.

Exhibits 4-1, 4-2, and 4-3 provide examples of the types of materials distributed during these meetings. Exhibit 4-1 sets out the responsibilities of the participants, helping to provide them direction regarding their roles and responsibilities. Exhibit 4-2 describes effective behavior by the leader or facilitator, who may be referred to as coach or a mentor. Many organizations like this idea because it employs a more informal, supportive title and helps break down the barriers to effective group teamwork. Exhibit 4-3 provides some useful guidelines for facilitating Q team meetings and keeping things moving.

Exhibit 4-1. Effective team member behavior.

1. Come to each meeting with an open mind and a willingness to cooperate.
2. If there have been any assignments made prior to the meeting, have the completed materials with you.
3. Before getting into any discussion, let the person running the meeting state the objectives of the meeting and what he or she would like to accomplish during this time period.
4. Listen carefully to what is going on, and where possible provide additional information or suggestions.
5. If the meeting starts to drift away from its objectives, work to refocus the direction by using tactful behavior. Focus on issues, not people. For example, don't say, "You're wasting our time." Say, "I think that idea is beyond the scope of our objectives."
6. When someone contributes a useful idea, tell the person so. The effective use of praise encourages more useful ideas and maintains a positive environment.
7. Get to know the other members of the group and what they are good at doing and not good at doing. Use this information to help the chairperson make assignments, so that everyone is focusing on strengths.
8. Try not to dominate the meeting. Give others a chance to speak and contribute while you play a passive role.
9. When you convey your ideas, look around the table at the other members so that it is obvious you are incorporating them into your comments.
10. When someone else is speaking, if you are not taking notes, look at the person and give him or her positive feedback. Nod, smile, or if appropriate, say, "Yes," or "I see," or "Right."
11. If there is a disagreement over some matter, focus the disagreement on what is said, not who said it. For example, say, "That suggestion is going to cost at least $1,000 and take three weeks to implement," as opposed to saying, "Your idea is a bad one."
12. Before the meeting is over, be sure that you clearly understand what you have to do between now and the next meeting. This will ensure that you continue to be a productive member of the group.

Exhibit 4-2. Coaching and mentoring.

A good team leader is also a coach and a mentor.

A coach is an individual who tactfully provides group members with helpful instruction and direction regarding how things can be done more effectively and efficiently. The focus of the coach is often on work-related matters, and in this capacity the individual tries to get everyone to play an active role as a team member.

A mentor is a person who offers advice and counsel designed to help the other person interact more effectively with group members and deal with problem areas, sometimes of a personal nature, such as the inability to get along well with another team member. A mentor often plays the role of counselor, adviser, guru, and all-around "wise person."

The following approaches are useful in coaching and mentoring:

1. Help in goal setting.
2. Get everyone on the team involved in the work.
3. Keep track of progress.
4. Manage conflict carefully.
5. Learn how to praise and/or correct without criticizing.
6. Listen carefully.
7. When required, keep information that is shared with you confidential.
8. Focus on helping the team members do a better job of carrying out their tasks rather than doing these things for the members.
9. Get to know the team members, and learn what tasks each is good at doing (and which tasks they perform poorly).
10. Work to build a team rather than a loose collection of individuals who are all working on the same project.

Develop a Feedback System

The QC needs to know what the teams are doing, so it is important to develop a feedback system for reporting progress. One of the ways to do this is to assign a Q team member to keep the minutes of the meetings and have them written up and distributed. These minutes are often less than two pages long and can contain as few as three major parts: (1) the date and time of the meeting, (2) a list of who was present or absent, and (3) a summary of what was said. If the minute taker has a lot of activities to report, the discussion can be broken into subparts by labeling each. A copy of the min-

(text continues on page 82)

Exhibit 4-3. Team facilitation guidelines.

A facilitator is an individual who keeps the group focused on the problem under review. When facilitating group activities, use the following guidelines to help direct your actions:

1. Make sure that problems or issues are clearly identified. Help the group define or describe what they are trying to do. Facilitate a focus.

2. If the group seems to be having problems coming up with solutions, focus their efforts by asking questions and reviewing the direction in which their responses are going.

3. Where possible, encourage the group to use brainstorming techniques.

4. During discussions, write down what everyone is saying. In this way, you have a list that you can work with later when thinking about what else you can do to encourage facilitation.

5. Keep the meeting positive. If someone starts complaining, ask the individual, ''What can be done to deal with this problem?''

6. Note the role played by each person in the group. Some individuals are better at identifying problems and some more effective at coming up with ideas for problem solving. Discuss these roles with the group leader because this is useful information when assigning tasks to team members.

7. Be sure that someone in the group keeps formal notes of what is being discussed and agreed upon, so that there is an action plan to be followed between this meeting and the next. If no one is taking notes, ask the group, ''By the way, who is taking notes today?'' This stops you from taking the play away from the group leader (because you are not giving an order), while ensuring that this function (note taking) is performed.

8. Try to be empathetic with the members of the group while viewing their opinions and statements objectively. This is useful in helping the meeting stay on track and make progress.

9. Be prepared to offer suggestions or comments where needed. Try to do this in the form of questions: ''What specific issue are we going to investigate for the next meeting?'' or ''I'm not sure I understand. How are we going to collect information on this problem?'' Play the role of a person who needs clarification and guidance, and use the word *we*.

10. Encourage everyone to speak or contribute by asking questions such as, ''I know that four of you agree with the recommended solution, but I was wondering if the other two members of the

group have a different idea. Is this the case?" "I was wondering how much agreement we have regarding the cause of this problem. Could you tell me again what you think is creating the problem and why you feel this way?"

11. Sit on the side or at the back of the group. Do not sit up front, or you will take the authority away from the group leader who is running the meeting. (You will appear to be a co-chairperson or have shared leadership authority with the formal leader.)

12. Meet with the group leader before and after the meeting to share your ideas with this person and get some feedback from him or her regarding what needs to be done. This understanding will help you facilitate without getting in the group leader's way.

13. Try to maintain the group's momentum by making positive comments on how well they are doing and the progress that has been achieved. Also, encourage the group leader to have everyone in attendance every time and remain aware of any slippage caused by people getting bored with the group meetings or not doing their assignments or contributing to the meetings. When this happens, it may be a good time to suggest to the group leader that a replacement person is needed. This is especially true if the group has worked together on two or three problems and is beginning to fall into a rut. Rotating members to another team often perks them up and gets them going again. However, this is a decision that should be made by the group leader working in cooperation with the quality council or whatever other group is chosen to assign people to the teams.

14. Arrive on time for all meetings, and have your homework done. The group leader is the focal point of attention during these meetings, but everyone notices when the facilitator is not prepared because this person is expected to jump in and help out when things start to bog down.

15. Try to work yourself out of the job. Set an objective of getting the group to work without your being there. A well-functioning total quality improvement team should be able to facilitate its own progress. As this begins to happen, your role diminishes, and you can become more of an observer and less of a "nudger." You are still needed in the meetings, but your role is a much smaller one.

utes can then be sent to the QC for review. Some organizations supplement the minutes with a one-page progress report that is easy to read and helps the QC members to keep up to date. Exhibit 4-4 shows an example of a progress report.

Look at Specific Examples of What Other Organizations Have Done

The ideas presented thus far should give you some idea of the considerations that go into organizing a TQM effort. Now let's look at specific examples of how award-winning companies have organized their quality programs. Each example is singular in its own way, but each is similar to the others too. As you read note the approaches that seem to be of most value to your own company.

Mayport Naval Station: Keep It Simple

Mayport Naval Station is an example of a straightforward, uncomplicated organizational approach to TQM. Its quality improvement structure consists of only five groups: a steering committee, quality management boards with accompanying process action teams, and quality improvement boards with associated quality improvement teams. (Exhibit 4-5).

The executive steering committee comprises the top-ranking officer at the naval station and other senior-level officers. This committee's job is to identify external customer requirements, develop and deploy the overall TQM plan, provide the necessary resources and decision support for seeing that the plan is implemented, and establish the quality management boards and quality improvement councils.

The quality management boards are responsible for improving processes that cut across departmental lines. The process action teams, which the boards help create and supervise, are responsible for carrying out these activities. The quality improvement boards are responsible for improving processes within their own departments. They create and supervise quality improvement teams to work on better processes.

The Mayport organization design is fairly simple, but it never-

Exhibit 4-4. Weekly Inner-Q Team Progress Report: Henry Lee Company.

HENRY LEE COMPANY
WEEKLY INNER-Q TEAM PROGRESS REPORT

Team Leader: _____   Meeting Date: _____

Task _____

_____

A) What Was Discussed?

    1. _____

    2. _____

    3. _____

B) What Was Accomplished?

    1. _____

    2. _____

    3. _____

C) Member Assignments:

    1. _____

    2. _____

    3. _____

    4. _____

    5. _____

    6. _____

    7. _____

D) Goal(s) for Next Meeting:

    1. _____

    2. _____

    3. _____

E) Date/Time of Next Meeting: _____

Send to vp of division w/ a copy of minutes every Friday.
If meeting was not held please include reason.
(Use the back of this form for additional comments.)

Source: The Henry Lee Company.

Exhibit 4-5. Mayport Naval Station quality improvement organization structure.

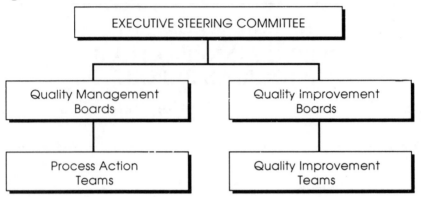

theless contains three characteristics that are common to virtually all TQM organizing efforts: (1) a council that is responsible for directing the overall effort, (2) teams that address both interdepartmental and intradepartmental issues, and (3) a system for evaluating progress and keeping the focus on continuous improvement.

AIL Systems, Inc.: Get Everyone Involved

AIL Systems, Inc. also uses a fairly simple approach to organizing its TQM efforts (Exhibit 4-6). The company president directly supervises both the functional organizations and the TQM Executive Council (TQMEC). Both of these groups have TQM committees under their direction.

The TQMEC, responsible for directing the formation of all AIL 2000/TQM teams, is headed by the president and comprises eight executives from various company operations. The group is responsible for identifying and setting priorities for TQM projects, allocating funds where needed, and providing overall review and control of the AIL/2000 quality initiative.

The AIL/TQM teams are assigned specific projects and present periodic reports to the executive council. In helping to ensure that each group is functioning properly, every team has a steering committee, which consists of at least two people from the TQMEC who support the group's work and provide guidance and direction. Additionally, a full-time facilitator is assigned to each group. This person, who has been trained in both TQM techniques and

Exhibit 4-6. AIL Systems, Inc., TQM operating structure.

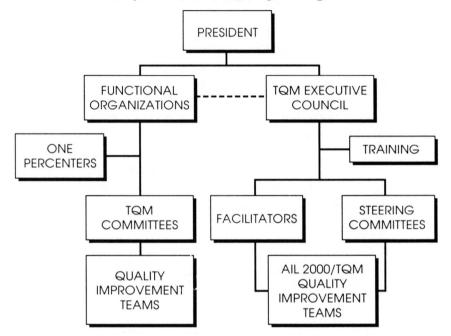

group facilitation methods, is responsible for helping the team focus on its goals. At the same time, the company's functional organizations have created quality improvement teams to help implement TQM in their own operations. These teams are assisted by what the company calls "One Percenters," employees who communicate with each other, discuss how to improve working conditions and operating efficiency, and act directly to implement the improvements. The term "one percenter" is common in TQM terminology and is used to reinforce the idea that if everyone does one percent more work, and does it right, quality will improve.

AIL's organization structure is similar to that used by Naval Station Mayport. It has (1) a council that is responsible for directing the overall effort, (2) teams that work on intradepartmental or special projects, and (3) a system for evaluating progress.

Blue Cross and Blue Shield of Arizona: Reinforce Your Philosophy

Blue Cross and Blue Shield of Arizona (BCBSAZ) offers a more sophisticated, comprehensive view of a TQM structure. The organization has carefully thought through its mission, philosophy, and objectives and has incorporated them into what it calls an ETQ (excellence through quality) triangle, which depicts the three components of TQM, supported by the four principles of the ETQ process (Exhibit 4-7).

The three components of the ETQ process are:

1. Quality planning, designed to concentrate BCBSAZ's efforts and resources on a small number of priority issues: increasing performance levels, improving communication among departments, and getting everyone in the organization involved in the development and attainment of goals.
2. Quality teams designed to provide a structured environment for employees to work together in improving the

Exhibit 4-7. The Excellence Through Quality Triangle (ETQ) of Blue Cross and Blue Shield of Arizona.

Excellence Through Quality

*Plan = do = check = act work philosophy.

Courtesy: Blue Cross and Blue Shield of Arizona.

quality of products and services, developing their job-related skills and abilities, promoting communication and teamwork, and improving the quality of work life.

3. Quality operations, designed to achieve consistency in operations as well as results, clarify individual responsibilities that contribute to achieving customer satisfaction, improve daily operations, and maintain the gains that are achieved through improvement projects.

These three components are supported by four principles:

1. Respect for people, which includes listening carefully to others, being respectful of them, and having a willingness to work toward solutions that benefit everyone.
2. Customer satisfaction, which refers not only to satisfying the needs and reasonable expectations of customers but also having a philosophy that puts the needs of the customer first.
3. Management by fact, which refers to the need to make decisions based on objective data.
4. Carrying out the PDCA (plan, do, check, act) work philosophy—that is, plan what is to be done, do it, check the results, and act to prevent errors or to improve the process.

The company's organizational structure looks elaborate (Exhibit 4-8), but a careful review reveals a design similar to that used by the Naval Station Mayport and AIL. The TQM effort is headed by a QC that is responsible for establishing ETQ objectives and policies, directing the implementation of total quality throughout the organization, evaluating progress, and supporting the overall process through recognition and reward efforts. This council meets monthly and consists of a director of quality service and members of senior management who represent a cross-section of BCBSAZ. Reporting directly to the QC is the design team, which is responsible for creating an implementation plan, and the executive division lead team, which provides support for lead teams.

Throughout the structure are a number of different types of Q teams, many of them similar to those used by AIL and Mayport Naval Station—for example, (1) functional teams that select and

Exhibit 4-8. The ETQ organization structure of Blue Cross and Blue Shield of Arizona.

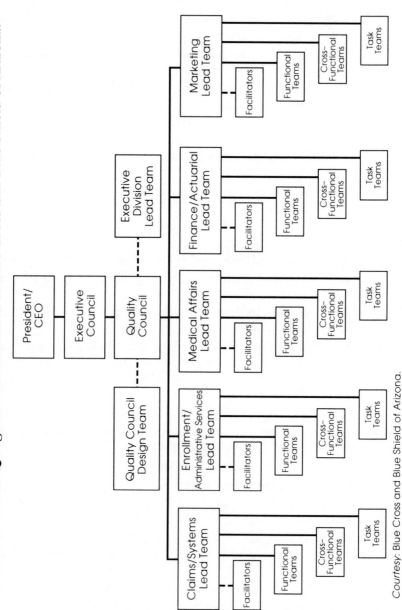

Courtesy: Blue Cross and Blue Shield of Arizona.

work on projects or improvement opportunities within their own department; (2) cross-functional teams that have members from more than one functional area and work on improvement opportunities that cut across functional lines; (3) task teams that have members from one or more functional areas and are formed to solve a specific problem or group of problems and are then disbanded; and (4) lead teams, which include management employees who set guidelines, handle logistics and communications, provide resources, and review solutions for the project teams but are not involved in problem solving itself. In addition, there are facilitators who support the coordination, implementation, and maintenance of the ETQ process at the team level.

The BCBSAZ structure may look somewhat foreboding, but remember that it is fairly simple in nature. The three characteristics that are uniform to these TQM organizing efforts are all present: (1) a council that is responsible for directing the overall program, (2) Q teams that address both interdepartmental and intradepartmental issues, and (3) a system for evaluating progress and keeping the focus on continuous improvement.

Perkin-Elmer: Tie It to Your Vision

Another good example of how to organize the TQM effort is by tying it closely to the company vision. Exhibit 4-9 shows how Perkin-Elmer has done this by using its vision and mission as the basis for formulating a strategic quality plan. From here, the company developed the organization structure for implementing the plan. The basics of this structure are illustrated in Exhibit 4-10.

The first step in organizing its quality effort was the formation of a quality steering committee (QSC), composed of senior executives who helped create the vision and mission statements and who now oversee the total quality process. Most members of the QSC also serve as project managers for one or more of the company's quality objectives.

The next step was for each quality objective project manager to develop a project plan by setting measurable quality objectives and getting these approved by the QSC. This individual is also responsible for managing progress and providing quarterly reports to the committee.

Exhibit 4-9. Perkin-Elmer's strategic quality plan.

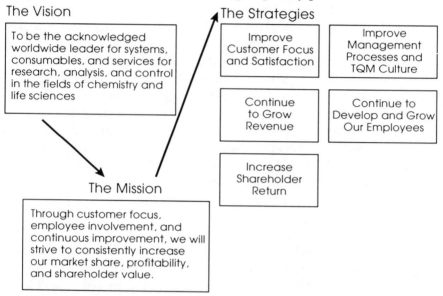

The Vision

To be the acknowledged worldwide leader for systems, consumables, and services for research, analysis, and control in the fields of chemistry and life sciences

The Mission

Through customer focus, employee involvement, and continuous improvement, we will strive to consistently increase our market share, profitability, and shareholder value.

The Strategies

Improve Customer Focus and Satisfaction

Improve Management Processes and TQM Culture

Continue to Grow Revenue

Continue to Develop and Grow Our Employees

Increase Shareholder Return

Perkin-Elmer also uses a series of councils and teams to help out in this process (see Exhibit 4-10) including worldwide councils, achieving competitive excellence (ACE) teams, plan of action (POA) teams, employee involvement (EI) teams, and quality infrastructure task teams. These councils and teams are important parts of the company's total quality structure because they provide a wide array of assistance in many critical areas. Infrastructure task teams are a good example. There are six: three that deal with people-related issues and three that deal with performance-related issues.

One of the people-related infrastructure task teams is the communication team, which is responsible for keeping all employees and external audiences aware of the goals, actions, and accomplishments of the company's total quality process. A second is the training team, which provides the tools and materials necessary to motivate and educate employees so that they can participate as active, contributing members. The third is the recognition and rewards team, which helps provide a structure that encourages all employees to enthusiastically pursue continuous improvement through both individual and team efforts.

Exhibit 4-10. Perkin-Elmer's quality organization structure.

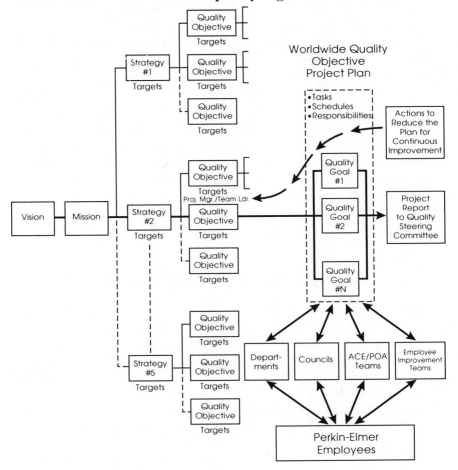

One of the performance-related infrastructure task teams is the benchmarking team, which continuously monitors the performance, practices, and processes of the competition, and shares this information with the quality teams so that they can improve their own operations. A second is the customer satisfaction assessment team, which is responsible for encouraging departments to carry out customer satisfaction assessment by collecting, collating, and analyzing customer feedback and helping the departments clearly understand customer needs both now and in the future.

The third is the quality measurements team, which is responsible for establishing metrics that will enable company personnel to improve the quality of their processes and performance.

Perkin-Elmer's approach is more sophisticated and detailed than any of the others presented here. Not all companies need this many committees. However, like these others, the company's arrangement is based on three essential characteristics: (1) overall direction, (2) the use of quality teams, and (3) a system of feedback that supports continuous improvement. Additionally, the company's approach helps illustrate that as a company gains more experience in pursuing total quality goals, it can devise more organizational systems to help support the effort. The use of infrastructure teams would not be very helpful for companies just setting up a TQM program. But for those trying to revise and streamline their programs, it serves as a useful model.

Design Your Own Structure

You now have enough information to start designing your own structure. Use the following worksheet. Make enough copies of it for associates who will be assisting you in this project. Take some time to consider each question, write down your preliminary ideas, and set a time for meeting with the other group members to discuss your responses.

Formulating a Total Quality Management Structure

1. Who will head the overall quality effort? What will be this person's responsibilities?

2. Will there be a quality council or committee to help out? If so, what will be its responsibilities? If not, will the person heading the overall

effort have the time and resources for doing the job? (In answering this last question, review answer to Question 1.)

3. What types of quality teams will be used? Functional? Cross-functional? Special task? Whatever one(s) are chosen, what will be the responsibilities of the respective groups? Briefly detail them.

4. How will progress be reported by each of the teams? To whom will these reports be communicated? Who will be responsible for the evaluation and monitoring of quality team progress? After describing this process in detail, does it dovetail with your other three answers or do some of the latter now need to be reconsidered?

When you meet to discuss your responses, be sure to allocate at least 20 minutes to each question. It is particularly important to address the last question because as you begin deciding the type of feedback you will need to monitor the process, you will often find that some of your initial organizing ideas are no longer valid.

In particular, remember that one of the major mistakes many companies make is that they overorganize their TQM efforts and find that they cannot monitor what is going on without spending an inordinate amount of time and resources. Let me give you an example.

One medium-sized company recently called me in to look over its TQM structure and offer suggestions for refinement. It had sent all of its top managers to a one-week TQM program offered by a major university. When the officers returned, they began implementing one of the rules they had learned: Identify your key performance areas, and assign a team to work with each. The problem was that the company identified eighteen key areas and assigned an average of 10 people to each team—and there are two manufacturing facilities in the organization. This meant that 360 people—out of 409 in the entire organization—were serving on TQM teams in the initial stages of the program. Just about everyone was either assigned to a TQM team or, as in the case of senior-level management, was a member of the QC.

On paper, the organizing effort looked good: Everyone was involved and there were eighteen quality teams at work. The problem was that this company had no way of monitoring so many teams and keeping control of the process. If it had thought through its answers to Question 4 in the worksheet, it would have identified this problem and realized that it had to start with a simpler structure that involved far fewer people. Then, after it had gained experience, it could have expanded the structure to include more people.

As you formulate your initial approach, keep two basic TQM principles in mind:

1. *Simplicity.* Design the structure so that it is easy to understand and implement.
2. *Clarity.* Make sure that everyone who is involved knows what they are supposed to be doing and that they have the time and tools to do it.

Remember that your first efforts are likely to require revision, but use them as a learning experience. Then, as things start to run smoothly, you can expand the structure, create more Q teams, and involve more people. Of course, these steps all assume that the associates are ready to hit the ground running. So before you actually get people involved in Q team efforts, you should provide them the training they will need.

5

Train the Personnel—With Simple, Practical, Profitable Tools

Most associates try hard to work efficiently. One reason that they sometimes fail is that they lack the right type of training. They do not know how to identify problems, or they lack the skills for analyzing these problems and formulating solutions. This is where training comes into the TQM picture.

One of the most common components of TQM training is statistical process control (SPC). This term is almost guaranteed to scare people away from training because it conjures up images of complex mathematical formulas and sophisticated sampling techniques. In most cases, fortunately, the needed training is far simpler and more easily understood by the associates. In this chapter, we examine a carefully selected handful of TQM tools and techniques most commonly used by the companies I studied. Some of them, especially those in manufacturing, go far beyond what I explain here, and if you discover this is what your organization must do, then you will have to continue on from where the chapter leaves off. But in most cases the ideas in this chapter will get you far down the TQM road, and without a great deal of time or effort for your associates to master these types of training. Basically, there are four steps to consider:

First   Carefully plan the initial phase of the training by
            starting slowly, getting everyone's support, and
            introducing tools and techniques that can be

	profitably used in just about every phase of the TQM effort.
Second	Teach the associates to collect and analyze data by choosing TQM tools that are easy to understand and can be used on the job to identify and solve quality-related problems.
Third	Combine, modify, and adapt TQM tools so that they fit the specific needs of your own organization, and your associates can effectively and profitably apply them to their own work problems.
Fourth	Design the training strategy and program so that (1) the associates are supportive of the program; (2) the first phases of the training are fairly simple, while more sophisticated training is reserved until later; (3) the training is applications oriented, and all participants can take the information back to the job and use it; and (4) at the end of the training, there is some type of reward for all the participants.

Focus on Problem Solving

There is no universal agreement on how TQM training should begin. Some organizations start with a social hour coupled with a brief explanation of the upcoming training sessions. Next, they give all participants a calculator and spend most of the remaining meeting time discussing how to use the machine. Before concluding, the individuals are given an assignment to complete back on the job (such as to determine how many customer service calls they receive each hour, which hours of the day are the busiest, and how long it takes them to complete the average call), and use their calculator to enter these data. Other businesses begin the training by providing participants with an overview of TQM and get them involved in discussing some of the changes that will have to occur over the next couple of years if the company is to remain competitive. The objective is to illustrate why a TQM approach is becoming increasingly important and why their support is needed.

Both of these avenues have two initial objectives: (1) to create the right climate for the training by giving initial support and (2) to link the training to its mission and profit goals (for example, "It will better help us serve our customers," or "It will help us maintain our position as the highest-quality provider of power supplies"). The important thing is not to start too fast or raise expectations too high, because this will lead to problems later on.

Some Useful Guidelines

However you introduce your own TQM training, start slowly and build interest and enthusiasm among the participants. In doing so, there are a number of useful guidelines to consider.

1. Before offering any TQM training, determine the length and scope of the program. What will be covered in each seminar? How many sessions will be conducted? How long will each session last? Who will be trained?

2. Sequence the training so that the simplest material is presented first and the most complex training is at the tail end. This organization will help build participant momentum and motivation.

3. Design each program or module so the participants have an opportunity to apply the information to their own job. If problem-solving techniques are being taught, make them relevant to the trainees or have these people bring in job-related information that can be addressed with the tools and techniques that are being studied.

4. Limit each training session to no more than twenty-five people. Otherwise the opportunity to ask questions and get feedback will be diminished.

5. Be sure to have all senior-level staff participate in the first training program to emphasize the organization's commitment to TQM. If nothing else, the managers will be able to answer TQM-related questions and play an active role in supporting the effort,

since they have been through the same training and understand what is going on.

6. In getting the specific type of training you need, consider designing your own programs in-house. If you feel you lack the expertise, bring in knowledgeable outsiders, but limit their stay. If they are going to be presenting the same material to more than three or four different groups, consider hiring them on a "train-the-trainer" basis, so you or some of your associates can conduct the rest of the training.

Training Types

Two types of training that are particularly popular in the early stages are problem solving and brainstorming.

Problem Solving

Problem solving is of fundamental value to TQM. Participants need to be able to identify problems and to distinguish between causes and effects. And while this may sound somewhat simple, many associates have difficulty. This initial training session can be a good place to start.

The most common approach is to walk everyone through the problem-solving process, explaining each of the basic steps, and then give the participants a chance to apply this information to an actual problem. Although there is no universal agreement regarding the specific steps in this process, these seven are representative:

1. Select and define the problem.
2. Analyze the cause.
3. Explore alternative solutions.
4. Selection the alternative that appears to be best.
5. Implement the solution.
6. Monitor the results. If they are not as expected, go back to Step 4, and choose the next most likely alternative. If they are as expected, move on to Step 7.
7. Share the solution with others who can benefit from this information.

During this training session, the main focus is typically identifying problems and distinguishing between causes and effects. For example, if a customer calls and says that she has not received her package and it was due 2 hours ago, what is the problem? Once the participants have identified the cause, they can discuss ways of dealing with it and, hopefully, prevent the problem from recurring. This is where brainstorming comes in.

Brainstorming

Brainstorming is a group problem-solving technique that encourages collective thinking to create ideas. Its value lies in the fact that there may be more than one way to deal with a problem. Through brainstorming, individual ideas or thoughts are not only brought out but may spark new ideas or thoughts from others. Advocates of the process sometimes use "brainstorm" as an acronym for describing the ten benefits of this approach:

B-R-A-I-N-S-T-O-R-M

1. Brings out the most ideas in the shortest amount of time.
2. Reduces the need to give the "right" answers.
3. Allows the group to have fun.
4. Increases involvement and participation.
5. Nurtures positive thinking.
6. Solicits various ideas and concepts.
7. Tempers negative attitudes.
8. Omits criticism and evaluation of ideas.
9. Results in improved solutions.
10. Maximizes attainment of goals.

Brainstorming is fairly simple to use. After the group identifies a problem, one person is assigned to record all of the problem-solving ideas that are called out by the team members. Participants are encouraged to offer as many suggestions or recommendations as they can think of, regardless of how outlandish or wild they might seem. All group members are encouraged to participate, and they are free to build on the ideas being offered by others. The initial focus is on quantity. Then, after everyone has called out all of their ideas, the group begins paring down the suggestions and evaluating their usefulness in solving the problem.

There are a number of brainstorming methods that can be used to direct the flow and processing of ideas. For example, under a round-robin approach, each team member in turn contributes an idea, which is then recorded. This continues until all ideas have been exhausted. Another approach is freewheeling, in which team members call out their ideas freely and in random order, and these suggestions are written down. A third approach is to have each individual write his or her ideas on a slip of paper. The slips are collected and the ideas recorded.

Regardless of the approach employed, the process helps generate potential solutions. One of the suggestions is then chosen for implementation. If it does not solve the problem, the group goes back to the brainstorming list and chooses the next most likely solution. This process continues until the problem is solved or the suggested solutions prove useless and the group meets again to brainstorm new solutions.

Brainstorming can be integrated into a wide variety of problem-solving approaches. For this reason, it is often taught early in the TQM training process and then linked with other training tools and techniques, such as those that teach the associates how to collect and analyze data.

Teach Associates to Collect and Analyze Data

Of the TQM training programs that are excellent follow-ups to problem solving and brainstorming, here we will look at checksheets, Pareto charts, cause-and-effect diagrams, and flowcharts. Many firms include these programs in their training because they are nonstatistical and easy to understand and apply.

Checksheets

A checksheet is an easy-to-understand form or list that is used to collect data and to answer the question: How often are certain events happening? The major benefit of a checksheet is that it turns opinions into facts. Follow these four steps to put together a checksheet:

1. *Agree on what is to be observed,* so that all who are assigned to carry out this task are collecting data on the same event or outcome, and be specific. For example, do not say, "Collect information on the inefficient office staff" because there is likely to be disagreement regarding what *inefficient* means. Instead, settle on a specific statement that will focus efforts, such as, "We will keep track of the accuracy of word processing among the office staff by identifying specific problems and errors in their work."

2. *Agree on a specific time period for collecting the information.* For example, it might be collected every day from 9 A.M. until 10 A.M. and 2 P.M. to 3 P.M. for 2 weeks in succession. Or it might be collected during these time periods on Monday, Wednesday, and Friday for 4 weeks in a row beginning next Monday. Deciding when to collect the information hinges on determining the best time for identifying quality problems. Sometimes the answer calls for random collection of data; in other cases, the collection focuses on specific days or times. (In the case of auto manufacturers, many people would argue that Mondays and Fridays are the best days because this is when quality tends to slip the most.)

3. *Draw up a checksheet form with specific criteria that identify various aspects of what the group wants to know about.* It is important to make sure all of the columns are clearly labeled and enough space is left to enter the data.

4. *Consistently and honestly collect the data.* This means making sure that there is sufficient time for getting all of the information, and the data are properly entered on the checksheet.

Exhibit 5-1 displays a problem and error checksheet that was used to evaluate word processing mistakes in the administration department of a business organization. This is an example of a particularly well-designed checksheet. The time period during which the information was gathered is clearly indicated, as are the purpose of the checksheet, the name of the person who collected

Exhibit 5-1. Checksheet for collecting information on word processing problems and errors.

Time Period: *July 11–15, 1995*   Date: *8/2/95*
Purpose: *Determine typing mistakes*   Name: *A. Sawyer*
in administration dept.   Department: *Administration*

Problem/Error	July					Total	%
	11	**12**	**13**	**14**	**15**		
Bold Lettering	///	//	////	//	///	14	5%
Centering	//	/	//	/	///	9	4%
Incorrect Page Numbers	/	//	/	/	/	6	2%
Missed Paragraphs	//	//	/	//	/	8	3%
Punctuation	⫶⫶⫶ //	⫶⫶⫶⫶⫶	⫶⫶⫶⫶ ///	⫶⫶⫶⫶⫶ ⫶	⫶⫶⫶⫶ ///	98	38%
Spacing	⫶⫶	////	⫶⫶ /	⫶⫶ //	///	25	10%
Spelling	⫶⫶ ////	⫶⫶ ⫶⫶	⫶⫶⫶ //	⫶⫶ ⫶⫶	⫶⫶ ////	55	21%
Tables	//	/		/	/	5	2%
Underlining	// ⫶⫶⫶	⫶⫶ /	⫶⫶ ///	⫶⫶ //	⫶⫶ //	40	15%
			Totals:			260	100%

the information, and the department in which the information was gathered. Even more helpful is the way in which the form has been designed. The problem or error has been clearly stated, the number of times each occurred has been noted along with the date of occurrence, the total number of mistakes has been calculated, and the percentage that each problem or error category represents has been determined. This checksheet reveals that punctuation is the major error. If the company can resolve this problem, 38 percent of word processing mistakes will be eliminated.

The fundamentals of a well-designed checksheet that are illustrated in Exhibit 5-1 can be applied to any problem your company would like to investigate. For example, if employee punctuality is the problem, the first step is to decide what constitutes punctuality. The second step is to determine how to identify the occurrence of this behavior, when and where to gather the data (for example, have someone note the number of people who come into the office after starting time in the morning), and for how long (for example, every day for 10 days in a row). Or a group might study customer service by looking at all of the customer surveys, note what customers do not like about the service, and sort the answers by category or response, such as the number of times people say it took too long to get service, the employee was not knowledgeable regarding the product line, or the salesperson was rude or condescending.

This type of approach helps the group identify the problems that are occurring most frequently and those that appear to be of minor concern. A good follow-up to this data collection procedure is the use of Pareto charts, which are often employed in tandem with checksheets and provide a simple, direct method of analyzing the data.

Pareto Charts

A Pareto chart is a form of vertical bar graph that identifies the relative impact of various problems. This simple tool is usually employed to count and then display the number of defects or problems of various types over a certain period of time. The technique helps delineate the relatively few categories or causes that typically account for the most problems. The steps in constructing a Pareto chart are fairly basic. As applied to the problem discussed for the checksheet in Exhibit 5-1, they are:

1. Identify the purpose of the data collection. In this case, determine how word processing productivity in the administrative department can be increased by reducing mistakes.

2. Determine the unit(s) of measurement, that is, identify the types of mistakes that are being made.

3. Decide the time period to be studied, that is, when the information is to be collected.

4. Gather the information.

5. Tally the data, and rank them by both category and number of occurrences. In other words, determine how many times each type of mistake has been made.

6. Determine the frequency of each category relative to all of the others, and rank the information in terms of this frequency. Exhibit 5-2 shows how this would be done for the word processing problem.

7. Graph the information, with the vertical axis displaying the range of frequency (or whatever other quantitative variable is being measured such as time or cost) and the horizontal axis containing bar charts for each of the major categories. See Exhibit 5-3.

Exhibit 5-2. Frequency and percentage breakdown of the checksheet data in Exhibit 5-1.

Problem/Error	Frequency	Percentage
Punctuation	98	38
Spelling	55	21
Underlining	40	15
Spacing	25	10
Bold lettering	14	5
Centering	9	4
Missed paragraphs	8	3
Incorrect page numbers	6	2
Tables	5	2

The bar charts should extend from left to right on the horizontal axis in order of decreasing frequency.

8. Starting with the bar chart at the left (the tallest one), draw a line that shows the cumulative frequency of all categories. Exhibit 5-3 provides an illustration of how this would be done using the data in Exhibit 5-2. Notice that the upward sloping line is a running total of the percentage of occurrences accounted for by the nine errors. Punctuation accounts for 38 percent of all mistakes; punctuation and spelling mistakes account for 59 percent of all errors; punctuation, spelling, and underlining account for 74 percent of all mistakes; and so on.

This simple process provides the basis for quickly identifying the most common problems and setting the stage for taking action. In the case of the word processing problem, the team would seek to answer the question: How can punctuation mistakes be eliminated? When this was done, the team would next tackle the task of

Exhibit 5-3. Pareto chart of word processing mistakes shown in Exhibit 5-1.

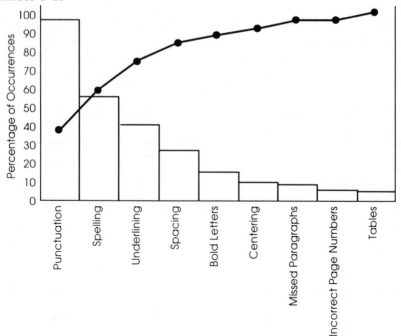

reducing spelling errors. This process would continue until the team had reduced all of the major problems and errors shown in Exhibit 5-1. Then the group would again collect data to determine the major word processing problems at this time, if any, and the process would start anew.

In the example, some mistakes collectively accounted for a substantial percentage of all errors. For example, the three most common mistakes represented 74 percent of all errors, and if the fourth most common mistake were included, the total rises to 84 percent. So by correcting fewer than half of all the types of mistakes, the group could reduce more than 80 percent of all the errors. This is one of the primary benefits to Pareto analysis: It helps focus attention on the small number of errors that are creating a large percentage of the problems.

Another benefit of Pareto analysis is that it permits manipulation of the data, so if the information does not provide any useful conclusions when examined in one way, it is often possible to realign the data to view them in a different way. For example, Exhibit 5-4 shows three types of data on client complaints: type of complaint, the facility at which the complaint was lodged, and the time of day when the complaint was made. A close look at these three Pareto charts shows that (1) no one type of complaint is much more prevalent than any other, (2) each of the four facilities is receiving an equal number of client complaints, and (3) significantly more complaints are being lodged later in the workday and significantly fewer earlier in the day. Thus, the last chart provides the best insights into improving client satisfaction. Now the team investigat-

Exhibit 5-4. Pareto analysis based on client complaints: searching for potential causes.

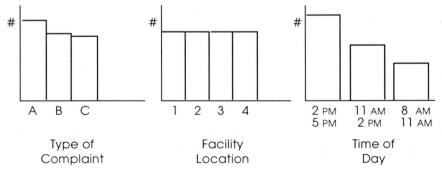

ing this problem needs to answer the question: Why are there more complaints later in the day?

Once this training is complete, many companies introduce the participants to cause-and-effect diagrams, which are particularly useful in generating potential solutions and are an excellent follow-on to Pareto analysis.

Cause-and-Effect Diagrams

Cause-and-effect diagrams are used to study the relationship between problems and their possible causes. The purpose of these diagrams is to illustrate clearly the various causes, sort these causes into major categories, decide which category offers the greatest potential for resolving the problem, and formulate a plan of action for dealing with this cause. This is done through four steps:

1. Identify the potential causes of the problem. This is usually done by having the members of the Q team brainstorm the problem, with one member writing down all of the responses.
2. Categorize the causes or place them into groups. For example, if the team is analyzing the reasons for unproductive meetings, it might conclude that one of the major problem categories is "time," and within this category are such reasons as: (1) People arrive late for the meeting, (2) the meeting runs over time, or (3) people have to leave the meeting before it is over. The group might conclude that "procedure" is another major category, and within this category are such reasons as: (1) There is no agenda, (2) people do not understand the purpose of the meeting, and (3) the participants do not stick to the agenda.
3. A cause-and-effect diagram is constructed by placing the problem statement in a box at the right of the diagram. (Exhibit 5-5 provides an example.) Then a horizontal line is drawn from this box to the left, and all of the categories and reasons within each category are placed in the diagram. Notice that if all the words were removed from Exhibit 5-5, the skeletal diagram would look something like a fish, hence the nickname "fishbone." (If there is a large number

Exhibit 5-5. A cause-and-effect diagram for dealing with unproductive meetings.

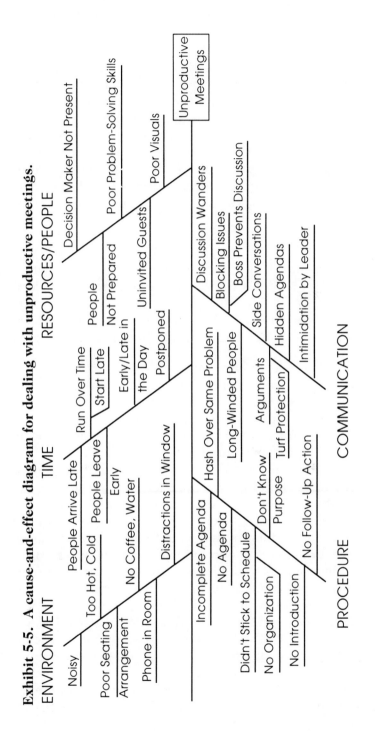

of major categories, the fishbone outline is more clearly seen, while if there are only two or three categories, the diagram does not literally live up to its name.)

4. The Q team then analyzes the diagram, decides which of the major categories is most likely to be causing the problem, and begins formulating a plan of attack. Sometimes this involves going back and getting more information; other times the group feels that it has sufficient data and can begin working on the problem immediately.

Flowcharts

A fourth commonly taught technique is the *flowchart*, which is a pictorial representation of the steps in a process. The objective of flowcharting is to examine all of the steps involved in carrying out a job, and then see if some of these can be eliminated or shortened, thus reducing cycle time. In flowcharting a process, there are eleven steps:

1. Brainstorm and record all of the steps that must be carried out in doing the job.
2. Put these steps in chronological order.
3. Put the proper symbol next to each step. (See Exhibit 5-6 for flowcharting symbols.)
4. Write the word START at the beginning of the flowchart.
5. Draw each required symbol and write the step inside. (See Exhibit 5-7 for an example.) When a decision must be made (a diamond box), there must be a "yes" or "no" to indicate what happens next in the process and this flow of activity must be connected back into the overall process.
6. Connect each symbol with a directional arrow to represent the sequence of activities. (See Exhibit 5-7.)
7. After the last step, write END.
8. Check the chart for correct flow and for any missing steps.
9. Go back to the beginning and assign times to each of the steps. When you are finished, add up the times and determine how long this job takes.
10. Review the flowchart and look for ways to eliminate or combine steps, and/or reduce the amount of time needed to carry out each step.

Exhibit 5-6. Flowcharting symbols.

 Operation: An action performed at one location. This step is represented by a box.

 Transportation (move): A step that moves the work or product from one workplace to another, either physically or electronically. This step is represented by a fat arrow.

 Inspection: A step where work is reviewed to make sure it is correct. This step is represented by a circle.

 Delay: A temporary stop built into a process. This step is represented by a large D shape.

 Storage: A step where material or data are held (physically or electronically) for later use. This step is represented by a downward-pointing triangle.

 Decision: Evaluates the process and provides options and must always have both a "yes" and a "no" exit. This step is represented by a diamond shape.

Direction of Flow: Denotes the direction and order of the process steps. This is represented by an arrow.

On-page Connector: Used to indicate that the flow is continued on another part of the page. This is represented by a shaded circle and letter. Corresponding letters indicate connection areas.

 Start: Denotes the beginning of the flowchart. This is represented by a shaded oval with the word START in it.

 End: Denotes the end of the flowchart. This is represented by a shaded oval with the word END in it.

Exhibit 5-7. A flowchart for writing a memo.

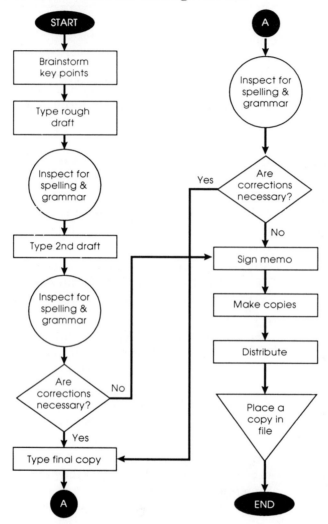

11. Draw the new flowchart with the accompanying times. Then calculate how much time has been saved with the new flowchart.

These four TQM tools—checksheets, Pareto charts, cause-and-effect diagrams, and flowcharts—are only some of the many that can help you increase quality. They are, however, the most commonly employed, and they certainly are among the simplest for training purposes. Of course, if others are needed, use them. Just remember to keep the focus on applicability and simplicity. For example, if you feel it is unnecessary to use the flowcharting symbols in Exhibit 5-6, drop them and flowchart your work processes by simply using boxes, lines, and arrows.

Combine and Adapt the Techniques to Your Own Operations

You can modify the wide variety of TQM tools to meet your organization's needs. We will look at two TQM-driven organizations that did this.

Wainwright Industries: Investigate and Correct

When investigating a problem, the first step is to gather information on it and then analyze the data. Wainwright Industries uses its Operation Readiness Report (ORR) form, shown in Exhibit 5-8, to handle customer problems. A close look at the form shows that the Q team is not only following all of the problem-solving steps described earlier in this chapter but is going beyond these steps. For example, in Step 3, the group is focusing attention on developing an interim correction action plan so that the customer's problem can be resolved as soon as possible. Then the group returns to the analysis of the root cause and works on developing a solution. A second focal point is prevention of recurrence (Step 7). A third is to reward the team by recognizing its collective efforts.

In completing all of the steps in the ORR Response form, the Q team could use checksheets, Parento charts, cause-and-effect diagrams, and possibly flowcharts.

If your goal is to identify and correct customer problems, think about how you could develop a form similar to that in Exhibit 5-8.

Baptist Hospital of Miami: Flowchart and Fishbone a Solution

In some cases Q teams can use their training to combine TQM tools and arrive at an optimal solution. This is what happened when

Exhibit 5-8. Quality team form for handling customer problems.

ORR#: _____   # Wainwright Industries Inc.   Date: _____
ORR Response Form

Description: _____

Customer No.: _____   Part No.: _____

Customer Name: _____   Originator: _____

1) Form Team:
   (A small group with the process/product knowledge, allocated time, authority and skill)

   _____

2) Describe Problem:
   (Identify in quantifiable terms the who, what, where, why, how, how many for this ORR)

   _____

   _____

3) Interim Corrective Action:
   (Isolate the customer from the problem within 24 hours)

   _____

   _____

4) Define Root Cause:
   (Identify all potential causes. Verify the root cause by testing each potential cause. Identify alternative corrective actions)

   _____

   _____

5) Permanent Corrective Action:
(Define and implement the best permanent corrective action. Choose ongoing controls to ensure the root cause is eliminated)

_____

_____

6) Verification:
(Quantitatively confirm that the selected corrective actions will resolve the problem without undesirable side effects)

_____

_____

7) Prevent Recurrence:
(Modify management systems, operating systems procedures, etc. to prevent recurrence of this and similar problems)

_____

_____

8) Congratulate Team:
(Recognize the collective efforts of the team)

_____

_____

Approval: _____ Date: _____

Courtesy: Wainwright Industries.

the Inventory Control Continuous Improvement Team at Baptist Hospital began investigating ways to reduce inventory.

After several brainstorming sessions, the group concluded that the current process was too cumbersome. Supplies from vendors were being sent to a warehouse and then transferred to a satellite inventory location, from which hospital inventory would be continually replenished. The team decided to investigate ways of reducing inventory and achieving operational efficiencies by streamlining the process for replenishing supplies in the satellite inventory.

Their first step was to flowchart the current inventory process (Exhibit 5-9). Then the group determined the time needed for each step, without using any of the flowcharting symbols. Armed with

Exhibit 5-9. Flowcharting an ongoing process: Baptist Hospital of Miami's inventory process.

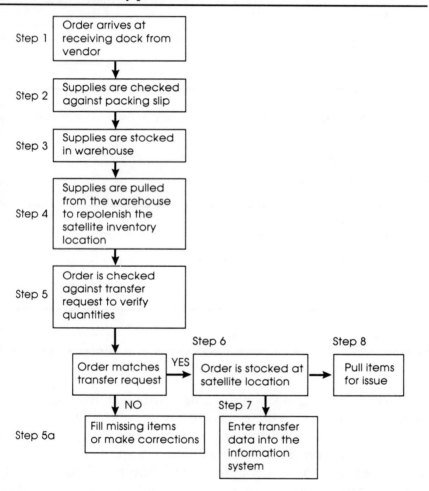

Process Flow Time Analysis

	Time per operation (minutes)	Weekly frequency	Total time/week
Step 2	30	3	1¹/₂ hours
Step 3	60	3	3 hours
Step 4	90	2	3 hours
Step 5	60	2	2 hours
Step 6	45	2	1¹/₂ hours
Step 7	30	2	1 hour
		Total	12 hours/week
			48 hours/month

Source: Baptist Hospital of Miami.

this information, the quality group began to brainstorm the reasons that satellite inventory replenishment took so long. They looked at four main categories: methods, manpower, materials, and machines. Based on an analysis of these causes, they constructed a new process flow diagram (Exhibit 5-10), and by following it reduced the time for replenishing inventory supplies by more than 70 percent.

The report in which the Q team details its analysis, solution, and results is presented in Exhibit 5-11. This type of report is extremely important because the QC (or the individual or other group that will make the final implementation decision) needs to review the team's approach and conclusions before allowing the team to proceed and complete the project. In this case, the recommendation resulted in a clear saving of both time and money, so the decision was easy. If the implementation had required the expenditure of thousands of dollars, the QC would have studied the proposal carefully and questioned the team's analysis and recommendations to ensure the requisite cost-benefit.

Design Your Own Training Program

To design your own training program, use the following worksheet. Photocopy it, and provide copies to those who will be help-

(text continues on page 121)

Exhibit 5-10. Fishbone and follow-on process flow analysis for Baptist Hospital's inventory process.

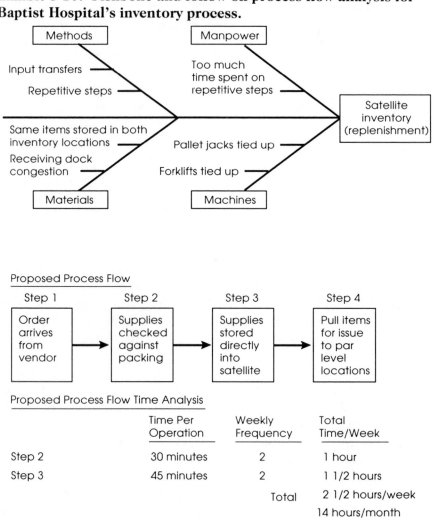

Exhibit 5-11. Continuous improvement report: Baptist Hospital's Inventory Control Continuous Improvement Team.

The Inventory Control CIT (Continuous Improvement Team) used brainstorming, process characterization, flowcharting, and data collection to implement improvements affecting the replenishment cycle for a satellite inventory location. The team was able to free up space that was previously occupied by 200 items in a bulk warehouse. There was a one-time reduction in the inventory value associated with those items. The process was reduced by 34 hours per month. The time gained was used to implement other programs designed to increase inventory accuracy and improve services to departments.

Project Selection

After several brainstorming sessions, the team came to the conclusion that one of the more cumbersome processes within the department's operation was the receipt of supplies from the vendors into the bulk warehouse, and the subsequent transfer of items from the bulk warehouse to a satellite inventory location. Supplies are pulled from this satellite location to replenish par level locations throughout the hospital. The team concluded, using brainstorming techniques, that the department had the potential for realizing major benefits if this process could be streamlined. The problem identified for study was defined in the following manner:

Reduce inventory and achieve operational efficiencies by streamlining the process for replenishing supplies in the satellite inventory.

Analysis

An analysis of the process characterization and fishbone diagrams showed that several steps in the process were repetitive. These included the initial physical receipt and checking against packing slips, the stocking of items in the bulk warehouse, pulling items from bulk, restocking into satellite location, verifying quantities before restocking, and pulling supplies from satellite for issue to par level locations. The total process took 9 hours and 30 minutes weekly, on average. Additionally, the department was ordering and receiving the items in question three times per week into the bulk warehouse, but replenishing the satellite location only twice per week. A backup supply for these items was maintained in the bulk warehouse.

(continues)

Exhibit 5-11. *(Continued)*

Solution

A process was designed to arrange for two deliveries per week to be received directly into the satellite inventory location. Since this would eliminate the backup supplies in the bulk warehouse, the vendor was brought into the process and asked to guarantee availability of product. The vendor was willing to do this, since it would be delivering these items twice per week instead of three times per week for the specific items that were no longer to be stocked in the bulk warehouse. A pilot program was set up, in which supplies in the bulk warehouse were maintained static, to provide backup during the trial period. Purchasing started ordering for the satellite location at a frequency of twice per week, based on on-hand stock status of the satellite location only, independent of the bulk warehouse quantities. Once the ordering pattern was established and the service level confirmed, enough confidence was built into the system to allow depletion of the duplicate inventory remaining in the bulk warehouse.

Results

The results were quantified in the following manner:

- Elimination of 200 items from the bulk warehouse location. Since items are directly received into the satellite location, there is no need to maintain duplicate inventories in the bulk location. Space freed up in the bulk warehouse as a result of the elimination of the 200 items will be used to bring into the official inventory items that are currently "unofficial inventory."
- There was a one-time saving on the value of the inventory in the bulk warehouse location. The average value was $40,000.
- There was a reduction in processing time of 34 hours per month in the Stores and Receiving Department. The value of the productivity gain is $311.10 per month, or $3,733.20 per year. The time gained has been used to improve services to requesting departments, to conduct additional cycle counts to ensure inventory accuracy, and to reduce the utilization of overtime in the department.

Courtesy: Baptist Hospital of Miami.

ing you with this exercise. Before you answer the questions on the worksheet, review the information in this chapter and take notes on the ways you can use training to increase quality.

Formulating a Training Strategy

1. What are the main quality problems facing our organization? Identify and describe them.

2. What type of training is needed in order to improve quality in our organization? Be specific.

3. How will we get this training that is needed? Who will receive it? Who will provide it? How much will it cost? How long will it take?

4. How will we evaluate the training? What types of measures will we

use? How will we know if the training is paying off? If it is not, how will we respond?

When you and your associates have completed this worksheet, meet to discuss what you believe needs to be done, when, and how. Based on this information, begin planning your training program, using the following six guidelines:

1. Prepare everyone in the organization for the training by offering a general orientation regarding why TQM training is needed and how it will be carried out. This strategy will help diffuse the rumor mill, which is likely to be passing on misinformation regarding the nature and purpose of the training.

2. Start the training with ideas that are easy to understand and use. Simplicity helps to reduce initial resistance and lays the groundwork for more sophisticated training later in the program.

3. Plan the program from beginning to end so that you know what needs to be done and in what order. If you simply offer training in a wide variety of tools and techniques that you think would be of value to the participants and do not think through how everything will be tied together, the program will end up being a hodge-podge of unrelated ideas and the associates will be disappointed in the program.

4. If you feel you lack the experience to plan the program or believe that it would be best to have the material presented by an outside expert, interview some consultants and trainers to find out what they recommend and how much they would charge you for their services. Be sure that these people have had experience in this

area before you hire them. Otherwise, you will end up paying them to learn what they have to teach to your staff—not what you want.

5, Be sure that the training is applications oriented, so it can be taken back to the job and used. When possible, have the participants gather information at the job site and bring it to the training sessions for analysis. This give-and-take between the training and the workplace is particularly helpful in reinforcing TQM ideas.

6. At the end of the training, provide some type of reward for all of the participants. This does not have to be expensive. It could be something as basic as a certificate that acknowledges that the individual received TQM training or a brief get-together for cake and coffee. You should attend this meeting in order to thank everyone for their participation, reinforce the importance of the training, and participate in celebrating their success. (More will be said about recognition and rewards in Chapter 7.)

Once the training is being applied on the job, you are in a position to evaluate how well things are going and to provide the associates with feedback on performance. Here is how an award-winning company carries out its training program.

CASE IN POINT

At Zytec, statistical process control training consists of a dozen training programs, preceded by an introductory meeting and wrapped up with a "What's next?" session. The fourteen meetings consist of the following:

1. Introduction to the calculator and math review.
2. Introduction to the class, including the course mission and an explanation of why all participants are being asked to attend.
3. An introduction to data collection, including the properties of good data collection, how to determine the data to collect, and types of collection sheets that can be used.
4. Training in sampling theory and techniques, including sampling methods, how to determine sample sizes, and how to carry out the sampling process.

5. Introduction to the use of graphing, including a discussion of the various types of graphs, how to choose the right graph, and guidelines for constructing graphs.

6. Training in Pareto analysis, including a discussion of the purpose of a Pareto chart and an exercise in constructing such a chart.

7. Training in cause-and-effect analysis, including the steps to use in constructing the chart, the questions to ask, and the process to use in conducting the analysis.

8. Introduction to the cause-and-effect diagram with the addition of cards, including the steps for implementation and how to tie this information into the adherence-improvement cycle.

9. Introduction to scatter diagrams, including common plot patterns, the use of scatter diagrams, and the construction of scatter diagrams.

10. Training in frequency distributions, including how to measure central tendency, construct a histogram, and check normality.

11. Training in variable control charts, including types of data, types of variation, and construction of an X bar and R chart.

12. Training in attribute control charts, including types of charts, advantages and disadvantages of these types of charts, and construction of the charts.

13. Introduction to process capability studies (PCS), including a discussion of what a PCS is, the four steps in a PCS study, and the difference between a PCS and a control chart.

14. Discussion of the "tool-box" concept, which emphasizes that in solving job-related problems, typically some statistical process control tools are better than others at addressing the problems, and these should be considered to the exclusion of the others.

6

Give and Get
Feedback—Easily
and Effectively

Feedback is critical to the success of every TQM effort. It lets you know how well your organization is doing and can help you formulate a strategy for dealing with any problems you uncover. Feedback also helps you keep associates informed and involved in the TQM effort.

The most common way of evaluating customer satisfaction is through the use of survey instruments. Examples were provided in Chapter 5. However, this is not the only approach. A simple technique such as management by walking around can be valuable in finding out what customers and associates like and dislike about how they are being treated. Another approach is to meet with associates daily or weekly to review the comments they hear from customers and give them an opportunity to make their own comments. But whatever you choose, the important thing is to develop a feedback mechanism.

The next step is to answer the "So what?" question: So what are you going to do about what you've learned? If the feedback is good, the answer is, "Keep on keeping on." If the information is not good, the answer is, "Develop a plan of action for correcting the problem and ensuring that it does not recur." Some of the ways of doing this will be examined in this chapter. So will ways in which you can keep everyone apprised of what is going on in the TQM effort and keep the associates motivated and willing to continue with their efforts. Basically, this process of giving and getting effective feedback can be achieved in four steps:

First   Evaluate customer satisfaction by getting objective feedback in all key areas of performance, such as your organization's promptness, friendliness, attitude, professionalism, delivery, services, quality, and community image.

Second   Work on ways to improve customer satisfaction, including dealing more effectively with complaints, anticipating client needs and setting up procedures for addressing them, and creating strategies for improving service.

Third   Keep associates informed and involved through the effective use of meetings, newsletters, and suggestion systems that promote feedback and serve as effective tools for praising associates and motivating everyone to continue their quality efforts.

Fourth   Design a personalized approach to giving and getting feedback in your own organization so that customer satisfaction continues to increase and strong associate support for the overall program is maintained.

Evaluate Customer Satisfaction

The primary reason for evaluating customer satisfaction is to answer the question: How well are we doing? The answer provides a basis for deciding what needs to be done, if anything.

The most common way to evaluate customer satisfaction is to ask customers to fill out questionnaires or other forms of feedback and then analyze these data. Here, you have two possible approaches: (1) Ask customers how well you are doing and compare this feedback to a predetermined level of performance, such as a goal of having 90 percent of all customers say that they feel your customer service is good or excellent, or (2) ask customers to compare your organization to some of your competitors and then look at how well you are doing in regard to these organizations.

One of the simplest ways of examining customer feedback is

to gather the information, quantify it, and compare the results to past performance. This procedure provides a straightforward way of determining customer satisfaction trends. Here are four case examples, ranging from fairly general to moderately detailed.

Phelps County Bank

At Phelps, one of the keys to success is customer satisfaction. After all, most customers could easily move their business to a competitor. In order to keep their business, Phelps stays in constant contact with each customer and continually assesses and monitors this relationship. Here are some of the actions it employs:

- Within ten days after opening a new account, the customer receives a call from the bank to ensure that he or she has received printed checks or a payment book and to find out if there are any concerns that need to be addressed.
- Six months after opening a deposit account, the customer receives a mail service survey. If the respondent supplied the bank his or her name or phone number, he or she receives a follow-up call.
- A customer who requests a particular service that the bank does not offer is given information about when that service might be available or an offer to help find it elsewhere.
- Three months after receiving a loan, the borrower is sent a customer survey. Any negative comments are addressed immediately or disseminated by electronic mail throughout the organization. As well, they are sent to the borrower's personal banker for follow-up.

These actions help Phelps identify and stay on top of customer problems. Other organizations follow a similar approach, often incorporating a greater degree of reliance on quantitative data.

Naval Station Mayport

Mayport is a federal facility that has many different types of customers, including naval personnel assigned to the base, spouses and children of these personnel, and visitors to the facility. The organization is determined to provide the highest quality of service to all of these individuals. One way is by measuring customer feedback on a periodic basis (usually annually) and using this information to see how well things are going. Here are some of their recent results that were reported in a variety of areas:

Automated Data Processing Department

	Yes	No
Did the department provide you with a knowledgeable solution?	97%	3%
Did the personnel act in a professional way?	100	0

Security Department

	Excellent	Very Good	Average	Poor
How would you rate the personnel on each of the following:				
Promptness	84%	13%	2%	1%
Friendliness	84	13	2	1
Attitude	83	8	6	3
Professionalism	91	6	0	3

Housing

	Strongly Agree	Agree	Disagree	Strongly Disagree
The police relate well to the kids?				
March 1993	10%	55%	17%	6%
September 1993	25	66	6	3
The police respond quickly to calls?				
March 1993	19	62	7	12
September 1993	18	72	5	5

Family Service Center

	1991	1992	1993
	(percentage responding yes)		
Did the center provide you with timely service?	60	69	92
Was the staff friendly?	85	88	96
Was the assistance you needed provided to you?	85	90	95

Valley Hospital Medical Center

Valley Hospital Medical Center of Las Vegas, Nevada, offers health and medical services to a wide range of clients. The hospital was founded almost twenty-five years ago, and now has a contingent of over 1,000 full-time and part-time associates. A few years ago, Valley recognized the need to implement an ongoing improvement program in order to ensure high-quality, competitive services. One area in which the hospital places major attention is customer satisfaction, although its approach differs somewhat from that of the Naval Station Mayport. Among other things, the hospital gathers data on the service provided by competitive hospitals and compares this to its own service levels. To do this, it gets responses from people who have been patients at Valley and also have had an inpatient stay at one of the other main area hospitals within the last two years. The information, collected by telephone survey, consists of answers to a series of sixty-one questions that address areas such as hospital satisfaction and outcome variables. Exhibit 6-1 shows the comparative information gained from a recent survey.

A close analysis of the data reveals that Valley's satisfaction score was significantly higher than Hospital A's in all categories except billing. The two largest differences were in the areas of nursing and admissions, where Valley's patients rated those services much higher than did Hospital A's patients. When compared to Hospital B, there were only a few areas where Valley had lower scores: ancillary services, hotel services, and privacy. However, Valley again has a higher overall satisfaction score and outcome average than did Hosptial B.

What is particularly useful in these comparisons is that they

Exhibit 6-1. Customer satisfaction analysis: hospital versus area competitors.

Satisfaction Scores	Valley	Hospital A	Hospital B
Nursing services	71.5	63.5	70.5
Admission procedures	70.3	61.0	66.5
Physicians	71.3	63.8	63.3
Discharge procedures	72.3	65.0	70.8
Billing	61.8	65.5	58.0
Ancillary services	75.3	72.3	76.3
Communication	71.3	65.0	66.0
Hotel services	66.8	64.3	70.5
Food	67.0	64.8	67.0
Privacy	66.3	61.5	69.8
Overall score	70.3	64.3	68.8
Outcome Scores			
Helped by admission	74.8	70.5	74.0
Community image	65.8	51.0	59.5
Quality of care	66.0	58.8	57.8
Brag about care	63.6	54.0	46.3
Recommend to family/friends	81.0	73.0	76.3
Return to hospital	80.8	75.0	74.0
Percentage dissatisfied	8.0	22.0	21.2
Outcome average	72.0	63.7	64.6

lend themselves to computer analysis, so is it possible to identify relations among the various factors. For example, Valley discovered that billing was a key factor in influencing the community image and quality of care scores. Similarly, admissions procedures and communication influenced the "recommend to family/friends" and "return to hospital" scores. By focusing on improving billing, admissions procedures, and quality of care, the hospital is working to improve its satisfaction score.

Wainwright Industries

Wainwright Industries builds precision parts and assembled systems ranging from computer disc drive covers to housings for electric motor applications and including seat belt, sunroof, anti-lock brake, power antenna, and power window mechanisms. Much of its work requires close tolerance machining, and its success depends heavily on customer satisfaction. Wainwright operates through the use of a specially designed customer satisfaction index (CSI) that looks at both internal and external customers and measures key perceptions in communication, delivery, quality, and service. These evaluations are then used in compiling an overall score. Exhibit 6-2 illustrates the combined CSI for the two groups for several years and targeted indexes for the future. In arriving at these ratings, Wainwright used a CSI survey, shown in Exhibit 6-3, that asked customers to rate the company's quality. In completing the instrument, customers use the following criteria in determining a score for communication, delivery, quality, and service:

Grade	%	Conditions	
A	100	Excellent	(meets expectations, no defect of any significance)
A−	90	Very good	(exceeds most expectations; minor problems; much better than average)
B+	85	Above average	(meets many requirements; no significant problems; all problem causes known and solutions under way)
B	80	Acceptable	(meets minimum expectations; problem causes known but solutions not developed)
B−	75	Below average	(misses significant expectations; progress is not clear)
C	50	Not acceptable	(needs major improvements; very dissatisfied with performance)
D	0	Very poor	(immediate corrective action required; critical flaws; cause of problems not recognized)

Based on the scores, an overall composite score is determined. Here are four scores and the overall composite from two surveys:

Exhibit 6-2. Customer satisfaction index for Wainwright Industries.

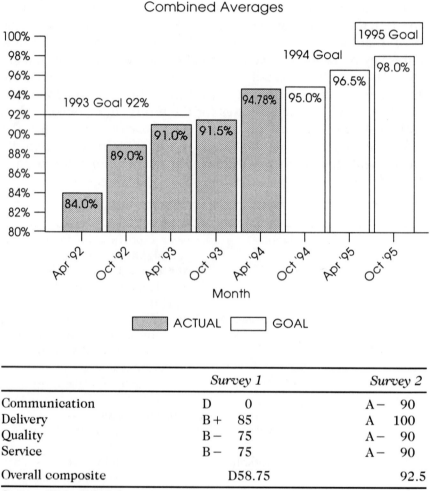

Combined Averages

1993 Goal 92%

1994 Goal

1995 Goal

84.0% · 89.0% · 91.0% · 91.5% · 94.78% · 95.0% · 96.5% · 98.0%

Apr '92 · Oct '92 · Apr '93 · Oct '93 · Apr '94 · Oct '94 · Apr '95 · Oct '95

Month

ACTUAL   GOAL

	Survey 1		Survey 2	
Communication	D	0	A –	90
Delivery	B +	85	A	100
Quality	B –	75	A –	90
Service	B –	75	A –	90
Overall composite	D58.75			92.5

Courtesy: Wainwright Industries.

Customers are also asked to provide comments regarding their evaluations. If the score is low, the survey results and comments are then turned over to special contact people, who are responsible for correcting these problems. In this way, corrective action is ensured.

Exhibit 6-3. Customer satisfaction index survey: Wainwright Industries.

Customer: _____   Contact: _____

Rating:

Communication	
Delivery	
Quality	
Service	

Rating Scale:

Grade	Conditions
A	Excellent
A−	Very good
B+	Above average
B	Acceptable
B−	Below average
C	Not acceptable
D	Very poor

Comments: _____

_____

_____

_____

_____

_____

Please return to us by _____

Thank you very much _____

Courtesy: Wainwright Industries.

Work to Improve Customer Satisfaction

In the previous example, Wainwright Industries used a follow-on strategy to address problems as they occurred and in the process improved customer satisfaction. Even in well-run organizations, regardless of the level of satisfaction, there are areas for improvement. Sometimes they involve correcting mistakes or dealing with complaints. Other times they focus on ways of improving performance.

Deal Effectively With Problem Situations

Common problem situations related to customer satisfaction are complaints by dissatisfied customers, decisions by customers to do business elsewhere (a sign that something may be wrong with the company's service), and dealing with somewhat tricky situations, such as shoplifting or children who are causing a ruckus in the store. Here are some of the ways that companies handle these situations.

Electronic Controls Company (ECCO)

ECCO, based in Boise, Idaho, designs, manufactures, and markets strobe lights for utility vehicles and backup alarms for trucks that beep when the driver shifts into reverse. The company's customer-service representatives, who field complaints, were authorized to write credit memos, ship replacement products or parts overnight, or do whatever else was necessary to keep the customer satisfied. However, ECCO decided that this was not enough. It needed to develop a system that helped identify and prevent problems from recurring. So the company decided to track problems and ensure that they were solved—once and for all. In doing so, ECCO developed a detailed approach for dealing with customer complaints. This approach encompasses a form, shown in Exhibit 6-4, that identifies the specific problem as well as the action that is being taken to correct it. This form has been designed to address virtually every possibility. Equally useful are the instructions that are provided to the associates, shown in Exhibit 6-5, so that they know exactly how to complete the form. This information covers everything the associate needs to know, including the objective of the form and the procedures for filling it out. As a result, associates can address complaints quickly and accurately.

Wild Oats

Wild Oats is a family of natural foods markets operating in Colorado and a few adjoining states. The company's purpose is to pro-

Exhibit 6-4. ECCO customer complaint form.

Leadership Team Review: _____ Mtg. Date _____

Production Team Review: _____ Mtg. Date: _____

Sales Team Review: _____ Mtg Date: _____

Copies Requested by: _____

Taken By: _____ Complaint Date: _____ Invoice #: _____ S.O.#: _____

Ship Date: _____ Customer P.O. #: _____

Customer: _____ Location: _____ Phone: _____

Contact Name: _____ ECCO Account Mgr.: _____

COMPLAINT: ☹ (Please Check)

PRODUCT LINE: ☐ Alarm   ☐ Light   ☐ Contract   ☐ Service

PRODUCT:
☐ Electrical interference
☐ Concern over early failure
☐ Warning labels missing
☐ No/wrong box labels
☐ Not boxed correctly
☐ Parts missing from kit
☐ Not labeled correctly
☐ Other:

SERVICE:
☐ Transit time too long
☐ Incorrect part shipped
☐ Out of inventory
☐ Short/over shipments
☐ Unit priced incorrectly
☐ Freight charge incorrect
☐ Sent order to wrong cust.
☐ Order not rec'd/entered

☐ Handling charge
☐ Incomplete shipment
☐ Competitive comparison
☐ Competitive pricing
☐ Past due shipment
DELIVERY:
☐ Error by carrier
☐ Other:

DETAILS:

FIRST RESPONSE CORRECTIVE ACTION: ☺

(continues)

Exhibit 6-4. *(Continued)*

MANAGEMENT REVIEW RESPONSE:
Suspected Root Cause:

☐ Track for trend (CLOSED)   ☐ No further corrective action required (CLOSED)
☐ Requires root cause analysis and further corrective action (OPEN)

CORRECTIVE ACTION TEAM:

ROOT CAUSE CORRECTIVE ACTION:

Complaint Closed: Date: _____   Authorization: _____
☺ ☺ ☺ ☺   Purge Date: _____

Courtesy: ECCO.

vide customers with the best selection of whole foods and health-care products, and to do so with an attitude that conveys friendliness, eagerness to serve, and readiness to educate. In carrying out these objectives, the company has developed useful strategies for dealing with customer complaints or awkward situations. These are spelled out in the company's staff handbook, which all associates are required to read. Here are some examples of how to handle customer complaints:

> If a customer has a complaint about anything concerning our operation, put them in immediate contact with a manager or owner (owners' phone #s are on the bags). If the proper person is not available, get the customer's name and number and have the appropriate manager call him or her as soon as possible. **Take every suggestion and complaint very seriously.** On average, a dissatisfied customer will tell his or her horror story to ten other people. Thereby, a single lost customer can cost the company tens of thousands of dollars in lost sales over the years.
>
> *Here are some helpful steps to use when dealing with unhappy customers:*

Exhibit 6-5. Directions for handling customer complaints at ECCO.

I. Objective

To be able to take the first response action necessary to satisfy the customer, and then to document the complaint and begin the root-cause resolution process.

II. Materials Needed

Customer Complaint Form

III. General Information

When a complaint is received from a customer, the first priority is to determine and take whatever "first-response" action is necessary to satisfy the customer. Everyone on ECCO's Sales and Marketing team is empowered to do so.

This task will give guidelines to help determine the most appropriate first-response action to take in order to satisfy the customer. Because each customer and each situation is different, this is not a listing of exact problems and their required solutions. It is necessary for the person receiving the complaint to use his or her best judgment in determining an appropriate response.

Although every Sales and Marketing team member is empowered to satisfy each customer, a team member faced with a situation in which he or she does not feel comfortable may choose to involve a team member with more experience to help. This in no way limits the authority of the team member to satisfy the customer but allows him or her the necessary freedom to feel comfortable with the decision.

IV. Procedures

1. If a customer calls with a complaint, the first, and possibly most important, step is to listen carefully and completely to the person on the phone. Do not interrupt, even if you feel that you understand the problem from the beginning. Often an unhappy customer is merely looking for a place to vent frustration and will feel better when given the opportunity to do so.
2. *The customer is always right.* Even if you feel ECCO is not at fault for the customer's problem, the customer perceives us to be or wouldn't have called.

(continues)

Exhibit 6-5. *(Continued)*

---

3. Always apologize to the customer. This important gesture is often forgotten in the rush to resolve the situation. However, it is essential that we convey to the customer that we care and are sorry that our mistake has caused problems.
4. The next step is to determine the first-response action needed to resolve the customer's problem. It is important to involve the customer in this process. Our idea of what will satisfy the customer is often different from his or her's. Be sure to ask the customer if the recommended action will satisfy him or her. It is often helpful to allow the customer to choose the resolution by giving alternative solutions (i.e., immediate credit or immediate replacement).
5. Once the customer is satisfied with the first-response action, follow through with the commitments made *immediately*.
6. Fill out the customer complaint form as described in the Sales and Marketing Quality Manual. This will begin the customer complaint root-cause resolution process.

V. Input Requirements

None

VI. Output Generated

Completed Customer Complaint Form

Courtesy: ECCO.

> *Listen.* Let them relate their problem to you in its entirety without interruption. Empathize. Many people just want to get a problem off their chest by complaining to a sympathetic ear. Let them know that you appreciate their dilemma and understand their frustration. This is the most important step . . . a solution without empathy will not leave a customer feeling satisfied.
>
> *Apologize.* Let them know that we are sincerely sorry about the problem.
>
> *Fix it.* Ask the customer what we can do to make it right. Be creative. There are no formulas. Whenever possible, resolve the problem immediately, on the spot. Don't always call someone else. Remember, any staff person

is authorized to give a disgruntled customer up to $25 (in the form of a cash refund, gift certificate, etc.) to try to remedy the problem. If it is going to take more than that, please call the manager.

Thank them. Thank the customer for bringing the problem to our attention and giving us the opportunity to correct it. Statistics show that 90% of dissatisfied customers won't complain; they'll just shop somewhere else.

Remember: The customers might not always be right, but they should feel like they are.

The company also offers suggestions to its personnel regarding how to handle awkward situations such as dealing with children who are engaging in disruptive behavior. Noting that both children and their parents are to be made welcome and personnel should be sure to greet both groups, the staff handbook suggests the following guidelines:

If a child is running or climbing in the store, explain that he or she could get hurt and he or she needs to stop. Talk to the child in a calm voice.

If a child's parent is aware of the "ruckus" the child is causing and is ignoring the situation, call your manager on duty.

Never restrain or hold a child *unless* the child's safety is endangered or the child is causing serious property damage (i.e., throwing products or climbing on coolers).

Phelps County Bank

Phelps is a small bank that relies heavily on customer loyalty for its profits and growth. So it has developed a number of strategies to ensure that customers are given more than they expect—and in many cases, it's little things that make the difference. For example, most banks open at 9 A.M. and close at 3 P.M. Phelps opens at 8:55 A.M. and closes at 3:05 P.M. And customers who show up after closing hours are invited into a secure room and given the help they need. The bank also goes out of its way to deal with customer problem situations, some of them implemented *before* a problem or customer dissatisfaction has occurred:

- A customer who expresses dissatisfaction regarding a particular matter is immediately asked what he or she would like to see done to handle the situation. Any suggestion regarded as fair and reasonable is carried out.
- When the bank receives a call on credit regarding a customer who may be going elsewhere for a loan, the customer's personal banker immediately calls the customer to find out if the bank can help meet the current need.
- Every month, when customer service representatives receive a list of closed accounts of their customers, they personally contact these customers to find out if there was dissatisfaction with the account or service. This information is recorded.
- All scheduled loan reductions of $10,000 or more are reviewed by loan officers weekly to determine if loans are being paid off because a customer has gone to another lender or is dissatisfied with the current service. Loan officers also personally contact customers who have paid off a loan.

In addition, the bank takes steps to head off potential customer satisfaction problems. For example, when interest rates on home loans began to fall in 1992, the bank anticipated that customers might begin refinancing their mortgages at lower rates with other banks. In response, each loan officer personally called his or her customers and offered to set up an appointment to discuss how their loan might be refinanced and the rate lowered. As a result, the bank lost very few loans to other lenders, even when rates continued to drop for the next eighteen months.

Focus on Improvement

In addition to making bad situations better, companies need to develop customer satisfaction strategies that promote improved service. These strategies often revolve around training and guidelines designed to create customer delight, as the following examples show.

First Union National Bank of Florida

First Union personnel are taught how to interact effectively with customers by developing telephone customer contact skills and personal customer contact skills. Here are the steps for carrying out each of these activities:

Telephone Customer Contact Skills

1. Identify the bank (First Union) and the branch name (where you are located).
2. Use your first and last name.
3. Use the caller's name, if available.
4. If you have to transfer the caller, give this individual the person's name to whom he or she is being transferred.
5. Invite the caller into the branch.
6. Thank the caller.
7. Speak in a friendly tone of voice.
8. Speak in a clear and distinct manner.
9. Handle the caller's request satisfactorily.
10. Make the caller feel valued.

Personal Customer Contact Skills

1. Stand, shake hands, introduce yourself with first and last names.
2. Acknowledge or apologize for any wait.
3. Maintain good eye contact.
4. Smile
5. Use the customer's name.
6. Make a genuine effort to meet the customer's needs.
7. Ask questions to determine the customer's needs before selling products.
8. Ask for the sale.
9. Sell additional products or services.
10. Thank the customer.

These simple procedures can be extremely effective in creating a customer-driven atmosphere and making the individual feel that the bank truly values his or her business. And in going an additional step, bank associates are authorized to give courtesy cards that provide the customer with a selection of free services (Exhibit 6-6).

North Broward Hospital District

The North Broward Hospital District uses a similar approach to First Union's, setting forth steps that should be followed in promoting customer service:

1. Maintain eye contact.
2. Greet the customer by name, if at all possible; smile; and offer assistance.

Exhibit 6-6. First Union's courtesy card to provide customers with free service.

Customer Service

C O U R T E S Y   C A R D

This card is our way of showing you that we mean what we say—When it comes to service, everything matters. Please present this card to your Customer Service Representative. It entitles you to your choice of any one of the following.

• One Personal checkbook order at no charge
• Rebate of one bank service charge (up to $10)
• One year no fee rental on a 3x5 safe deposit box

Your satisfaction is important to us!

Offer good at the branch listed below when signed by the Branch Manager. Not valid with any other offer
FIRST UNION NATIONAL BANK OF FLORIDA

Branch Manager   By

Branch Name

Offer good thru

First Union National Bank
of Florida

Courtesy: First Union National Bank of Dade/Monroe County.

3. Maintain behavior and decorum appropriate to the situation.
4. Attend to customers immediately when they approach.
5. Notice when someone looks confused. Visitors who appear unfamiliar with their surroundings should be offered immediate assistance. If you do not know how to direct the visitor to the location they seek, find someone who does. If possible, escort them to their destination.
6. Do not conduct personal conversations in front of any customer.
7. Maintain patient confidentiality.
8. Do not gossip.
9. When answering the telephone, identify your department and yourself, and ask how you may be of assistance. Ensure that messages are delivered.
10. Let customers go first (in elevators, through doors, etc.).
11. Express concern to visibly angry customers. Try to obtain the facts about the situation and resolve the problem yourself or refer to the appropriate person for resolution.
12. Accept responsibility to attempt to solve a problem or address a complaint, rather than focusing on determining fault.
13. When something is needed that is not specifically or necessarily your job, help anyway or find someone who can.
14. Take the time to listen; it's the first step toward good communication.
15. Always remember that our customers are often under stress; do not let your bad day be reflected in your behavior toward them. They deserve courtesy and respect at all times.
16. Always address delays or situations where a customer will have to wait with a simple explanation. Address these situations as early on as possible.
17. Go out of your way to anticipate customer needs; go the extra mile to meet customer needs; put yourself in the customer's shoes.
18. At all times maintain a professional decorum. Remember, every employee is a representative of the entire organiza-

tion; therefore, you must look neat and professional at all times.

Wild Oats

Wild Oats guarantees 100 percent customer satisfaction and honors merchandise exchanges with no questions asked. When a customer wants a cash refund, the associate asks for a receipt, but if the person does not have one, the associate is urged to use his or her best judgment. The goal is to keep the customer satisfied, and if the person appears to have bought the item or is a regular customer, the sales associate will provide the refund.

Another example of Wild Oats's efforts to create customer satisfaction is provided by the guidelines in the company handbook given to associates regarding how to handle telephone and intercom communication:

> It is imperative that everyone answer the telephone quickly and courteously. Phones should never ring more than three times before being answered. Please answer the telephone, **"Hello, Wild Oats Market, this is** [give your name]. **How may I help you?"**

Here are some other phone tips:

- When getting a fellow staff member to help a customer, let the customer know that. Otherwise, the customer assumes you are checking on something for him/her and tells the staff person that picks up the phone that they have been helped already. We end up with an unhelped, annoyed customer.
- Follow up on a phone call to make sure the customer has been helped.

Do Not Leave Anyone on Terminal Hold!!!!

- Encourage the caller to leave a message. Be sure the message is clearly written and delivered promptly to the appropriate person. Do not ever tell a caller, "Can you call back in a few minutes?" Always take a message.

- When using the intercom, always speak clearly and repeat the message twice. Speak calmly and professionally.
- If the person being paged doesn't pick up immediately, take a message from the caller. The person he or she was trying to reach is most likely busy with a customer or out of the building. Do not page twice.
- Make personal calls only on your break and keep them short and infrequent in order to keep the lines open for business calls.
- Feel free to let the customers use our phones for quick, local calls.

Keep Associates Informed and Involved

Associates are also part of your customer base, and it is important to keep them informed and involved. Some of the most common approaches to keeping associates up-to-date are through meetings, newsletters, and employee suggestion systems. The following examples are drawn from companies that were surveyed for this book.

Wild Oats

Wild Oats places a major focus on communicating with the associates and, in turn, giving each an opportunity to express his or her opinions, suggestions, or complaints. The company believes that the process is essential in making everyone feel like a valuable member of the organization. This two-way flow of communication is promoted in a number of different ways. One is through monthly meetings between department managers and the staff and between the store managers and the department managers. Additionally, there are bimonthly all-store meetings for all staff members. These meetings are mandatory; anyone who cannot attend is required to get prior approval from the general manager. Full attendance helps ensure that everyone knows what is going on and that all questions are answered. Since the owners also come to these meetings whenever possible, there is a strong likelihood that those present will be assured that their concerns are being heard and will be acted on.

The home telephone numbers of the owners are printed on each store's grocery bags. The company's handbook notes, "If customers aren't shy about calling us at 6:00 A.M. on a Sunday morning, then you shouldn't be either. We hope that our store managers are dealing with any problems at the store level and we don't want to undermine their authority, but we recognize that at times the 'chain of command' may need to be circumvented."

Other forms of communication include staff surveys, which are made twice a year, and exit interviews, which are held with people leaving the company. The purpose of this feedback is to determine how well things are going and to identify better ways to manage the staff.

First Union National Bank of Florida

Newsletters can be a fairly time-consuming and sometimes expensive form of communication; often they are used only by larger organizations or those that have had a TQM strategy in place for at least a couple of years. Nevertheless, they are an excellent form of employee communication and can be both informational and motivational.

A recent First Union newsletter reported the results of the latest customer survey, pointing out areas where the bank received good marks and those where improvements are needed:

1. Overall, customers are very satisfied with the service they are receiving.
2. Fewer than 1 in 12 (8%) rate the bank's service as poor.
3. The vast majority (91%) who left a message for a call back were satisfied with the service from the Message Center Representative.
4. But, one-quarter of the customers (23%) are unhappy with the amount of time that they wait for service when they call the branch.
5. The second most common problem is dissatisfaction with waiting time in branches (15% rated as poor).

The newsletter then set out the survey conclusions and recommendations for action. As a result, associates were made aware of where customer service was viewed positively, where customers felt service had to be improved, and steps that needed to be considered in accomplishing this goal.

First Union's newsletter also reports actions taken by associates to provide customer satisfaction. In these cases, the person's name is reported, followed by a brief description of something he or she did. Here is an example:

> **Maritza Frech,** Teller Supervisor at *Doral* was helping with the phones and received a call from someone inquiring about the bank. She was instrumental in setting up a call that resulted in the sale of at least 17 products. (1 Business Account, 10 Personal, 2 PELs [Prime Equity Lines], 3 Mortgages, 1 IRA [Individual Retirement Account] and possible investment business.) *Way to go, Maritza!*

Still another benefit of the newsletter is the opportunity it provides to the employees to ask questions and provide input of their own (Exhibit 6-7). What better way to ensure that there is employee feedback than by asking the personnel to communicate?

Henry Lee Company

Henry Lee promotes communication by encouraging its personnel to submit quality-related ideas *and* letting them know the status of their suggestions. Henry Lee has done this with an extremely well-formulated approach. This approach sets forth the eligibility guidelines for submitting quality tips (Q-Tips, for short) and details the various categories of rewards. Associates who are interested in submitting a Q-Tip are asked to fill out a form on which they detail the problem they have identified, their suggestion for improvement, and the value of implementing the suggestion. The individual's Q-Tip is then evaluated, and a decision is made regarding its usefulness. All new Q-Tips are eligible for a prize.

In all, there are nine tiers of rewards and recognition. These are explained in Exhibit 6-8, which details what associates have to do to be eligible for an award and/or win one. A close reading of the table shows that the submission of a Q-Tip makes an individual

(text continues on page 151)

Exhibit 6-7. Soliciting employee feedback in First Union's newsletter.

QUESTIONS, COMMENTS, QUIPS & CONCERNS!!!

We want to hear from you! What's on your mind? What do you want to know? What's got you confused? What are you worried about? Got a rumor you want to dispel or confirm? Do you have a success story?

Simply fill this page with your thoughts and send it in or Fax or FUNmail it. We'll try to answer as many of your questions as we can, either through this newsletter, meetings, memos or other forms of communication.

Remember, the only way to find out . . . is to ask! The only way to let us know . . . is to tell us!!

_____

_____

_____

_____

_____

_____

_____

SEND OR FAX TO:
ANDREA MUSTELIER, FUNFACTS EDITOR, • FIRST UNION
FINANCIAL CENTER, FL6207,
FAX #789-4809 OR SEND YOUR MESSAGE BY FUNMAIL!

(All signed questions will receive a response. Unsigned questions will be answered—and all the answers published in FUNFacts—only if they are of general interests to First Union employees in Dade and Monroe).

Courtesy: First Union National Bank of Florida, Dade/Monroe Counties.

Exhibit 6-8. Shining Star Program at the Henry Lee Company.

What is it?
A reward system for the associates of Henry Lee.

Why does Henry Lee need a reward system?
The *new* environment at Henry Lee is about positive change. Henry Lee associates that courageously embrace and contribute to the *new* environment shall be rewarded as well as associates that go above and beyond the call of duty from their everyday duties.

How does an associate participate?
There are numerous ways for an associate to participate. A list has been provided below:

Q-TIP, Q-TIP Third Place, Q-TIP Second Place, Q-TIP First Place, Q-TIP Suggestion of the Year, Leadership Training Course, *Q-TEAM, *85%+ Attendance, *Inner Q-TEAM, *Q-STAFF member, Q-STAFF member as a Facilitator, *Sub Team, Implemented Recommendations (teams only), Customer Calls or Writes about an Associate, Associate to Associate, Star of the Month, *Recording Secretary, Team Leader (Q-TEAM, Inner Q-TEAM, Sub Team), Implemented Q-TIP

*associated with TIER III

Q-TIPS

TIER I	1 lottery ticket (25 monthly) awarded along with **5 point(s)** for every complete nonduplicated Q-TIP suggestion.
TIER II	**15 Point(s)** for implemented Q-TIPS awarded monthly along with the following cash prizes:

10 Points and $50.00 for Third Place
15 Points and $75.00 for Second Place
20 Points $125.00 and Associate of the Month parking spot for First Place
30 Points and a "Star burst" of cash for the "Suggestion of the Year"

TEAM PARTICIPATION

TIER III	Q-Team, Inner Q-Team, and Sub team. **15 Points** to associates for 85%+ attendance and participation for every team a person contributes on. In addition, a Q-STAFF member as a facilitator.

(continues)

Exhibit 6-8. *(Continued)*

Minutes of all the meetings held by one team determine the 85%+ requirement. A copy of the completed minutes provided for the TQM Coordinator.

IMPLEMENTED RECOMMENDATIONS

TIER IV   Certificates for all implemented recommendations presented by Q-Teams, Inner Q-Teams, and Sub teams. Certificates provided for all participants of Q-STAFF because they are the keepers of the Q-TREK system.

75 Points Q-STAFF	Certificate and "T" Shirt	Ex. A
	Annual luncheon with Ed Sternlieb	
25 Points Q-Team	Certificate and "T" Shirt	Ex. B
15 Points Inner Q-Team	Certificate	Ex. C
10 Points Sub team	Certificate	Ex. D

STAR OF THE MONTH

TIER V   **25 Points** awarded for the associate chosen by a vote of the steering committee. Henry Lee managers nominate any one associate for star of the month based on the set criteria. The steering committee votes for one associate based on the nominations the third Wednesday of the month.

The Q-TREK board features the star of the month.

TIER VI   **150 Points** earns an associate a $25.00 gift certificate for Publix.

TIER VII   **200 Points** earns an associate 1 Day off per year with pay.

ELITE CLUB

TIER VIII   **300 Points** earned inducts the associate into the **ELITE CLUB**. Members receive a $50.00 certificate for dinner (no alcohol), star pin and their name listed on a certificate with the other **ELITE CLUB** members to hang on the *Shining Stars of the Henry Lee Galaxy* wall.

PRESIDENT'S CLUB

TIER IX   **400 Points** put the associate at the pinnacle of TQM. Members are treated to a coordinated 1 night Hotel stay worth a maximum $150.00 (no alcohol). Members are given a star pin and their name listed on a certificate with the other *PRESIDENT'S CLUB* members to hang on the *Shining Stars of the Henry Lee Galaxy* wall.

Q-TREK BOARDS

A Q-TREK board located at all Henry Lee News stations tracks the following: all Q-Teams, Inner Q-Teams, Q-Tips, and Sub teams for every department. *Finance— Operations—Sales—Merchandising—Tampa—Orlando*

The TQM Coordinator will update these boards and keep a database on all associates' points earned from program participation.

The *Shining Stars of the Henry Lee Galaxy* will be an annual program. All awards presented annually with the exception of the Star of the month and Associate of the month.

Associates can give stars to other associates for going above and beyond the call of duty. "Who's your Lucky Star?" forms are available for anything positive.

Thank you for the hard work

You're really appreciated around here

That's a great idea

Great teamwork

Anything positive given to or received by anyone

These will be placed in the Q-TIP suggestion box or by leaving a message on the TQM's phonemail.

This program is at the sole discretion of the Henry Lee Company. The company reserves the right to change, modify or discontinue the program at any time with or without notification.

Courtesy: The Henry Lee Company.

eligible for a Tier I award and a lottery ticket, plus it earns the individual five points. As the person continues to participate in the TQM program and build up points, he or she can eventually end up in the President's Club (Tier IX). Moreover, while the program is comprehensive, and everyone has an opportunity to earn rewards, the program is not very expensive. Exhibit 6-9 provides an initial estimate of expenses for the Shining Star program. Quite clearly, the company has been able to provide a wide array of rewards at a very reasonable price, illustrating that quality award programs are easily within the financial grasp of any company.

This idea of tying communication feedback and rewards is

Exhibit 6-9. Estimate of expenses for the Shining Star Program at the Henry Lee Company.

Expense	Cost per Expense	Number of People	Total Expense	
TIER I Lotto Tickets	$1.00	300	300	
TIER II Prizes	$250.00	12	3,000	
"T" Shirts Q-Staff and Q-Teams	$152.00	5	760.00	Averaged over 5 years cost of $152.00 per year.
Q-Staff Annual Luncheon	$10.00	12	120	Estimated cost per Associate.
Gift Certificate to Publix	$25.00	30	750	Estimation of number of winners.
One Day Off With Pay	$106.23	15	1,593.45	Estimation of number of winners.
Dinner for Two (No Alcohol)	$50.00	10	500	Estimation of number of winners.
One Night Hotel Stay (No Alcohol)	$150.00	3	450	Estimation of number of winners.
Star Pins ($4.38 each)	$263.27	5	1,316.35	Average over 5 years cost of $263.27 per year.

Total   7,128.72

Source: The Henry Lee Company.

critical in helping to ensure that the associates continue to submit quality-driven suggestions. In fact, all successful TQM efforts have a recognition and reward system of some kind. Chapter 7 will address this topic in greater depth.

Design Your Own Approach to Getting and Giving Feedback

The examples presented in this chapter should provide you with more than enough information to design your own approach to gathering and evaluating customer satisfaction, as well as to decide how to provide information to your associates and get feedback from them. Review the questions in the following worksheet, which are designed to help you bring all of this information together in a logical, coherent way. On a separate piece of paper, jot down your initial thoughts regarding each answer. Then review the material in this chapter and use it to help you reformulate and reshape your answers. When you have completed this initial pass through the worksheet, make copies of it for everyone who will be helping you with this exercise and have them write out their own answers. Then set up a meeting to discuss how you will get your own feedback system in place.

Formulating an Effective System for Giving and Getting Feedback

1. How will we get customer feedback? How will we analyze it?

2. What types of strategies can we formulate to deal with customer complaints and related situations?

3. What steps will we take to ensure that associates remain informed and have a means for communicating back to us? If we include a newsletter in this process, what will be the format of the letter, and who will be responsible for producing it?

Remember that the material in this chapter cannot be implemented after one session of discussion. You will need to look carefully at all of the customer data you are gathering and brainstorm regarding how the information can be analyzed and interpreted. This may require you to meet once a week for 4 or 5 weeks. Similarly, when you are trying to determine how you will develop a strategy for maintaining customer satisfaction, you are likely to find that after the first couple of meetings, you have come up with a great number of ideas, but it will take you months to implement and evaluate all of them. The same is true regarding employee communication, since newsletters often require months of work before the first one is ever produced. And then there are often more months of changes as the newsletter begins to develop, dropping some initial types of information and adding others.

You must commit yourself to staying the course. Getting and giving feedback is an ongoing process, and you will continually find yourself revising your strategy.

7

Provide Recognition and Rewards—Let Your Associates Know You Care

A TQM adage holds,"What gets rewarded, gets done." This cliché helps drive home the point that many organizations make strong initial progress on their TQM journey, but these efforts soon run out of steam because the associates lose their enthusiasm for quality improvement. Why? One of the major reasons is that the personnel see no benefits for themselves. In analyzing why this happens, there are four important rules to keep in mind.

1. A recognition and reward system is vital for eliciting a strong initial response to your TQM program. Without one, the effort will be viewed as an attempt by management to profit at the expense of the associates.

2. Ensure that the system is motivational to personnel. What will get them to support the TQM effort? The right to park next to the main entrance? A cash certificate? A plaque? Each organization is unique, and recognition and rewards in one enterprise are often regarded as meaningless in others.

3. Make it possible for everyone to qualify and win. If you are tying your recognition and reward system directly to sales, the people in merchandising and shipping are unlikely to get behind your effort because there is nothing in it for them. A more broadly based system is needed, although this opportunity does not have to be equal across the board.

4. Do not overuse financial rewards or set them too high. Offering extremely large financial rewards takes the focus off quality

and puts it on money. Areas where associates can obtain large rewards are then given major attention, and the other areas are ignored. And when there eventually are no more large financial awards to be earned, enthusiasm for the program will wane.

The recognition and reward program must be designed to achieve TQM quality objectives and meet your unique needs. In achieving this objective, there are four steps:

First	Identify the types of rewards that are likely to be of most value to your associates and are acceptable to the organization.
Second	Communicate the reward and recognition system so everyone knows what they have to do to qualify for rewards and they are aware of how and when these are offered.
Third	Gather and chart feedback on how effective the reward and recognition system is working, so that appropriate changes can be made.
Fourth	Drawing upon these ideas, create a reward and recognition system that is designed to meet the unique demands of your own organization.

Identify Meaningful Rewards

In creating a system that meets the needs of your organization, it is helpful to examine some of the possible forms and rewards:

plaques	logo items (hats,	special luncheon
trophies	shirts, pens,	dinner with
certificates	mugs, coasters,	spouse or
CEO letter	etc.)	friend
honor roll	banner for office	trip (local or dis-
letter to person-	special parking	tant)
nel file	space	seminar atten-
picture in com-	introduction to	dance
pany news-	board	pick-your-own-

paper	lapel pin or jew-	gift
use of limousine	elry	catalog
savings bond		gift certificate
		day off
		cash
		tickets to special
		events

Most of these items cost the organization very little money. It is the recognition and psychological benefits that are most appealing, as many of the organizations highlighted in this book have found.

Most effective TQM organizations combine financial rewards and recognition into a well-designed system. It's all a matter of choosing the right mix. Here are some of the approaches of the award-winning companies I examined.

Wild Oats

Wild Oats offers a Moment of Truth Award, which honors staff members for performance above and beyond the call of duty. The award consists of a letter of recommendation that remains in the individual's personnel file and a $10 gift certificate that is usable at Wild Oats Marts. Any staff member can recommend another person for this award, and final approval is given by the general manager.

Mayport Naval Station

Mayport has a wide range of awards that are tied to both individual and team efforts:

- Letters of appreciation
- Eagle of Excellence certificates
- Cash awards
- Military medals
- Civil service awards
- Letters of commendation
- Articles in weekly naval station newspaper
- Articles in the monthly *TQL* (total quality leadership) *Newsletter*

- Presentation of TQL mugs
- Sailor of the Quarter
- Sailor of the Year
- Nonrated Person of the Year
- Junior Petty Officer of Quarter
- Sikorsky Maintenance Person of the Quarter
- Civilian of the Quarter
- Civilian of the Year
- Workcenter of the Quarter
- Performance awards
- Recognitions in family-gram newsletter
- Evaluations
- Positive counseling
- End-of-tour awards

These awards are presented in a number of forums, including awards ceremonies, departmental gatherings, and the senior leader's going to the job site to present the award to the individual. At Mayport there are few days in which employees are not given formal recognition or rewards.

Valley Hospital Medical Center

Valley has very strong feelings regarding the need to recognize and reward associates for outstanding performance, and there are a number of different awards. Some are standard fare, found in most other organizations—for example, increases in compensation and promotions, both based on performance reviews. In fact, over 80 percent of promotions at the hospital are given to in-house personnel based on superior performance. Among its other awards are these:

- Employee of the Month award, based on predetermined criteria and given to an individual selected by his or her peers
- Employee of the Year award, chosen from among the year's twelve Employee of the Month winners
- An annual awards banquet, where associates are recognized for their continued service to the hospital
- Longevity bonuses to reward employees for continued service and perfect attendance

- "Atta Boy" certificates, given to employees who go out of their way to assist a customer (Exhibit 7-1)

Valley gives all of its managers thank-you cards, which are used to thank associates for exceptional service, and employees are given thank-you cards to use in thanking other employees, departments, or outside agencies that have provided assistance to them.

Communicate to Everyone What Is Going On

A tailor-made recognition and reward system is a good beginning. But it is also important for everyone to know how the system works and be aware of who is being recognized and rewarded. Associates who understand the system will know how to get involved. If they know who is being rewarded, they may be motivated to participate.

Make Sure Everyone Knows the System

The reward and recognition system should be simple enough so that everyone understand how it works. Employees should also know the criteria for winning—or at least being considered for—awards.

Mayport Naval Station

The naval station offers a wide array of recognition and rewards to its associates. In getting them to pursue these awards, the organization sets out clear criteria for each one (Exhibit 7-2). Any civilian working at the naval facility who makes a significant accomplishment to organizational effectiveness is eligible for a special act award in the form of a cash payment. Any naval employee who exercises personal initiative and quality performance is eligible for a Sailor of the Year award. And everyone who works at the facility can receive a cash award for a benefit suggestion that results in cost avoidance, cost reduction, or process improvement. In addition, the

Exhibit 7-1. "Atta Boy" certificate at Valley Hospital Medical Center for employees who provide exceptional service to customers.

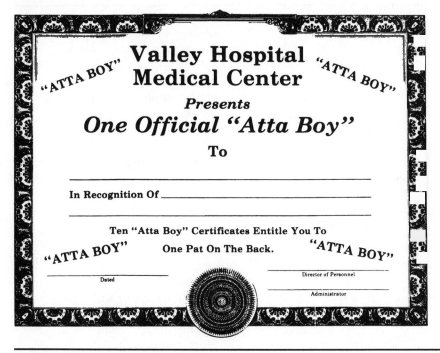

Courtesy: Valley Hospital Medical Center.

base newspaper and newsletters report noteworthy accomplishments.

The naval station communicates the methods by which employees can get involved in TQM efforts and thus qualify for recognition and rewards. Some examples are provided in Exhibit 7-3, which reports practices and the feedback mechanism associated with each. For example, individuals or groups interested in making cost-saving suggestions know that these suggestions will be acknowledged within 5 days by the local human resources satellite office, and the people who made them will be notified about the status of their suggestion, including whether it is accepted and im-

(text continues on page 165)

Exhibit 7-2. Awards and criteria: Mayport Naval Station.

Job Family	Award	Criteria
Civilian	Civilian of the Year/COY (incentive)	Outstanding performance enhancements through continuous improvement
	Civilian of the Quarter COQ (incentive)	Outstanding performance/ contribution
	Special act (incentive/ cash)	Significant accomplishment to organizational effectiveness
	Performance award (cash)	Outstanding work quality throughout appraisal cycle
	"On the spot" (cash)	Spontaneous recognition for quality performance
	Quality salary increase/ QSI (cash)	Basic pay increase based on outstanding performance
	Within-grade increase/ WGI (cash)	Basic pay increase based on performance
Military	Sailor of the Year/SOY (incentive)	Personal initiative and quality performance
	Sailor of the Quarter/ SOQ (incentive)	Personal initiative and quality performance
	Military medals, all ranks (incentive/ heroic)	Personal initiative and quality performance
All	TQL team awards	Demonstrated leadership in implementing TQL initiatives
	Eagle of Excellence	Peer recognition for quality contributions to daily work
	Beneficial suggestion/ Benny Sugg (cash)	Cost avoidance, cost reduction, process improvement
	Buy our spares smart/ Boss II (cash)	Cost avoidance, cost reduction, eliminate fraud and waste
	Letter of commendation	Meritorious contributions to the organization
	Letter of appreciation	Continuous contribution to the organization
	Gifts/plaques/lapel pins	Continuous service
	Newspaper/newsletter recognition	Noteworthy accomplishments

Exhibit 7-3. Quality practices and feedback mechanisms: Mayport Naval Station.

Practice	Participation	Feedback Mechanism
TQL process improvement input (PII) (NAVSTA suggestion program)	I/G	Receipt of employee suggestion logged. Written acceptance by commanding officer implementation decision; quality improvement award/ recognition
Navy-wide buy our spares smart (Boss II)	I/G	Immediate local feedback and management assistance for processing. Boss II office Philadelphia, PA acknowledges receipt w/in 1 week by letter and sends imprinted coffee mug just for suggestion submission. Monetary award/recognition.
Navy-wide beneficial suggestion (Benny Sugg)	I/G	Acknowledgment of employee suggestion w/in 5 days by local human resources satellite office (HRO) Jacksonville. Written acceptance/implementation decision.
Workforce surveys 1. TQL climate survey 2. Command climate assessment survey 3. CMEO survey	I	Results communicated in basewide publication; Mayport mirror-plan of the day; ESC, quality management board meetings. Command assessment team (CAT) and command training team (CTT) participate/develop follow-up activities.
Captain's calls (quarterly)	I/G	Open forum—question and answer sessions for all personnel.

(continues)

Exhibit 7-3. *(Continued)*

Practice	Participation	Feedback Mechanism
Quality awareness month	I/G	Recognition for commitment to quality via special luncheons, networking seminars, newspaper coverage and public recognition
Recognition programs Eagle of Excellence SOY/COY Letters of appreciation	I/G	Peer recognition/awards
Contributions to employee publications	I/G	Employee bylines—pictures
Improvement teams	G	Ongoing recognition—idea sharing via storyboard presentations
Weekly departmental quarters (all hands MTGS w/functional dept heads)	G	Employees meet with department head to discuss improvement opportunities
Employee participation in VIP tours/briefings	I/G	Immediate visible recognition as briefer/spokesperson for their work
Videotaped success stories	I/G	Immediate visible recognition disseminated activity-wide and ultimately navywide
Commanding officer's action line	I/G	Immediate acknowledgment of receipt of employee concern w/in 24 hrs.
Memorandum of understanding between NAVSTA Mayport and the American Federation of Government Employees Union (AFGE)	I/G	Continuous open commitment and support of TQL values and initiatives by the local union

Source: Mayport Naval Station.

plemented. Similarly, individuals serving on improvement teams are provided with ongoing recognition, and their ideas are shared with others throughout the facility. And those who make quality contributions to daily work and are recognized by their peers are eligible for such awards as the Eagle of Excellence, Sailor of the Year, Civilian of the Year, and letters of appreciation. A close comparison of Exhibits 7-2 and 7-3 shows that the two reinforce each other and help the naval station convey information related to the types of awards that are given and the criteria for receiving them.

Additionally, the naval station lets everyone know the awards that have been given, so it becomes obvious that these are achievable goals. For example, since June 1992 the following awards have been made:

Navy Achievement medals (special act): 28
Navy Achievement medals (sustained performance): 47
Navy Commendation medals: 20
Meritorious Service medals: 4
Legion of Merit: 1
Commanding officer letters of appreciation: 243
Flag letters of commendation: 27
Recommendations for Sailor of the Month/Quarter/Year: 51
Recommendations for Civilian of the Quarter: 24
Eagles of Excellence: 378
Civilian monetary: 194

Let Them Know Who Is Being Rewarded

It is also important to identify award winners. This practice gives the individuals well-earned recognition and reinforces the organization's message that quality efforts will be rewarded. The following shows how the Henry Lee Company and First Union National Bank of Florida, Dade and Monroe Counties, do this.

Henry Lee Company

Henry Lee follows an approach similar to that at Mayport. Through the use of an effective communication system, the personnel are kept apprised of TQM progress. This is done in a number of ways. One, explained in the previous chapter, is by giving rewards to those submitting quality-related ideas, as well as to those whose ideas are implemented. However, the company takes this idea even further, by also detailing eligibility for awards—and thus encouraging the personnel to continue their TQM efforts. An example is provided in Exhibit 7-4, where recognition is given to those who have submitted eligible Q-Tips. All of these individuals were given a lottery ticket as a prize and are eligible for a second-tier award, if their suggestion is implemented.

Exhibit 7-5 reports the results of Q-Tips that were implemented. These suggestions were all eligible for second- and fourth-tier awards (see Exhibit 6-8). The final decision regarding the awards is always made by the Q-staff at its next meeting. Once this is done, the winners are announced and the prizes are awarded. Henry Lee's communication process thus ensures that everyone learns the status of their contribution, knows the awards that are available, and is encouraged to continue contributing to the quality effort.

The financial awards are quite small; $125 per month is the largest for an implemented idea, and a Q-Tip that is eligible for implementation qualifies the individual only for a lottery ticket, which may prove to be worth nothing. Nevertheless, the company continues to get suggestions for improvements, illustrating that it is not large rewards that are the backbone of a successful TQM program but the enthusiasm and cooperation of the associates.

First Union National Bank of Florida

Among First Union's interesting approaches for recognizing and rewarding associates are SWATs (Start a Winning Attitude Team). The idea for SWATs was a result of a climate survey conducted among the associates in Dade County, Florida. An analysis of the results revealed that many unresolved employee issues, feelings, and concerns needed to be addressed, so the bank president, Carlos Migoya, created SWAT lunches, during which individuals could talk about what was going on in the company and what needed to be done.

The president began holding monthly luncheon meetings at

Exhibit 7-4. First-tier awards and recognition at the Henry Lee Company.

	Name	*Department*	*Q-Tips*
1	Richard White	Merchandising	2
2	David Stone	Warehouse	1
3	Niles Andersen	Warehouse	1
	Jose Gutierrez		
4	Brian Kluge	Mis	1
5	Tom O'Malley	Sales	2
6	Tim Haynes	Night Cashier	1
	Charles Smith		
	Edward Garcia		
7	Rene Morato	Night Cashier	2
8	Harold Waite	Warehouse	1
9	Martha DeHaven	Warehouse	1
10	Phil Powers	Customer Service	1
11	Louise Ackman	Transportation	1
12	Sara Fontana	Customer Service	1
13	Thomas Dunn	Customer Service	1
14	Paul Wilson	Merchandising	1
15	John Rodgers	Sales	1
16	Crystal Baer	Routing	1
17	Harvey Hide	Warehouse	1
18	Rick Washington	Warehouse	2
19	Karol King	Sales	3
20	Michael Ruoff	Customer Service	1

All Q-Tips listed above will receive a lottery ticket and have a chance to receive a 2nd tier reward once their suggestion is implemented.

We did receive many Q-Tips which were eligible and may even be implemented but had no names associated with them. Next time, take credit for your suggestions; it could be very rewarding!

Courtesy: The Henry Lee Company.

his nearby house and used this time to talk to small, informal focus groups of associates. These individuals were chosen at random from a list provided by the Payroll Department, with an effort made to get equal representation from each of the branches and departments. SWAT lunches now have fifteen attendees: ten from the previous meeting and five new members. Notes are taken at the

Exhibit 7-5. Implemented quality tips at the Henry Lee Company.

	Q-Tip	Written By	Referred To	Reply/Action Taken	Benefit
1	Picking stickers being placed over the label on individual spice containers making it difficult for customer to identify product	Mary Wright	Vice President Operations	Q-team formed and procedure established to properly place labels on products	Customer less frustrated when receiving and using products
2	Fumes and noise level from kitchen/lunchroom permeate second floor	Jose Rodríguez	Vice President Finance	Q-team formed to decide whether or not to close the door (just kidding)	Employees who work during lunch times able to concentrate now
3	Customers getting credit for items already received due to invoice procedure problem	Alan Klinger	Vice President Operations	Policy implemented by transportation manager which includes proper notation of invoice by both customer and driver	Money saved, less aggravation for customers and employees
4	Rainwater leaking between wall and sidewalk canopy between warehouse and building	Jean Bosch	Vice President Operations	Rain gutter installed	Do you have to ask?
5	Customer service missing item inquiry option while in order entry	Carmen Fuentes	Vice President Finance	Program corrected by MIS department	Much time saved in order entry when customer asks about a specific item during order

The above Q-Tips will be reviewed at the Q-Staff meeting on 9/28 and all recognition and rewards will be decided.

Courtesy: The Henry Lee Company.

monthly meeting, to ensure that nothing important is forgotten. At the same time, confidentiality is stressed, so everyone knows that they can speak their mind without having to be concerned about suffering a backlash. The results of these SWAT lunches are reported in the company newsletter, and this information provides input regarding how to improve operations. In addition, those attending the lunches are asked to share their thoughts about the program, and these comments are reported in the company newsletter. Here are some of the remarks that appeared in a recent newsletter:

> "Before I was invited to a SWAT meeting, my impression of FUNB [First Union National Bank] was that they only valued their customers and their employees didn't matter. At the first meeting I attended, Carlos Migoya opened the meeting by saying that the reason for the gathering was that he and FUNB care about the employees. He asked everyone how they felt about working at First Union. He told us that he and FUNB were concerned about how we felt. Carlos not only listened to our problems, he also made sure changes took place. I feel that the SWAT meetings made a lot of good things happen."

> "The experience that I have had with the SWAT meetings has been positive. I think whoever thought of the idea for SWAT was great. Upper management gets to hear the positives and the negatives of what is going on in the branches so that we can continue what we're doing or change it. We also get to listen to each other and get ideas from one another. Some of the issues we've discussed are improvements on our medical insurance and other benefits we have here at First Union."

> "I like discussing the problems with confidence. We need these meetings for information and it helps a lot."

> "I enjoy discussing what is on everybody's mind to let upper management know what is going on in the field."

> "The atmosphere was very pleasant. It provided for candid conversation and was in no way intimidating."

"It gives you a sense of understanding and is a nice way to express your thoughts about your overall feelings about your own branch."

"It was conducted in friendly atmosphere. Carlos was very open and candid in his response. Offering his home as the meeting place showed that he is committed to a family-type of institution."

SWAT progress is reported in the quarterly newsletter, as is SWAT talk (comments from those who attend these luncheons). In addition, the names of individuals who are SWAT team members are published, so they receive recognition for their contributions.

Recall from Chapter 6 that First Union singles out individuals in the newsletter for outstanding performance. Here are two examples that illustrate how effective communication can be used not just to give feedback but to provide recognition as well:

Recently *Business Banking* saved a loan at the closing table. **Lourdes Arias,** Vice President and account officer, received a call from the bank's attorney saying that further approvals would be needed due to some easements from FPL [the local utility]. The customer had given them 15 minutes and walked out of the closing. Lourdes worked with the attorneys and **Steve Leth** and **Jess Lawhorn** to get the needed exception. The attorneys got the customers out of the elevator to close on a $1.35 MM new loan. *Great job, Lourdes!*

Amy Cid, a *Private Banking Assistant,* is doing a great job in customer service. She recently assumed responsibilities over the Hold Mail, and her diligent efforts have resulted in a business customer retrieving over $5,000 in long forgotten accounts which had returned mail and were dormant for over a year. **Keep up the good work, Amy!**

A third way that First Union uses communication is to familiarize the associates with newly implemented quality-driven programs, to keep them alert to new developments and help build their support for these efforts. For example, the bank recently introduced the ":05 or $5 in '95" program, designed to reduce the amount of time that customers have to stand in teller lines. If a person is in line for more than five minutes, the individual's account is credited for $5. The program was first discussed in 1993, developed in 1994, and implemented in 1995. In ensuring that it was able to meet the demands of the program, First Union analyzed factors that were obstacles to serving customers in five minutes or less. Prior to the ":05 or $5 in '95" program, it frequently took six to eight weeks to hire, train, and replace tellers. First Union implemented a hire-ahead program to ensure that all teller positions are filled more quickly. The hiring function moved from the individual branch managers to a county-wide service manager. The bank's roving teller staff was increased and centralized. Substitute teachers from Dade County Public Schools were trained as tellers. In addition to being "on call" to the county's schools, these teachers are "on call" to First Union Dade County branches to fill in for unexpected teller absences. Finally, the composition of the teller staffing has changed to more part-time employees and fewer full time. This allows more flexibility in having tellers working during the hours they are needed to better meet customer traffic patterns. And this helps ensure that all branches have adequate tellers, something that will be critical to making ":05 or $5 in '95" work effectively.

The bank continues to communicate its quality philosophy to associates, so that they are aware of changes. For example, the president recently announced two new programs designed to improve customer service. After describing the programs, he tied them to the main theme of customer services by noting:

> We will be selling by "servicing" our customers. If all we did is match our products to our customers' needs with each and every opportunity we get—our sales would triple, our customers would feel valued, and YOU would feel proud of your achievements.
>
> As we go into [the new programs], let's take a positive outlook on our new skills, and make sure we practice them as often as opportunities arise. Remember, one of the most important parts of our Vision is to make our

customers feel *so* valued that they rely on First Union for all their financial needs. If we focus on our Vision, we can't help but be successful.

Get Feedback on Results

It's not enough to offer recognition and rewards. There must be an evaluation of the system's effectiveness. Is it producing the desired results? If not, what needs to be done? One way to answer this question is to gather and chart data on performance.

The gathering of data ensures that the organization is managing by fact. The charting of the information helps the enterprise track performance over time and make comparisons with both its own past performance and that of the competition.

Wainwright Industries

Wainwright encourages its employees to submit ideas for improving operations. Data from the company's recent Baldrige quality award application show how well it is doing in this area.

The average number of implemented suggestions submitted annually was 54.7. In comparison, the average for the typical American company is 0.3, and for the typical Japanese company, it is 12. Obviously Wainwright's response is very good. It is not unreasonable to assume that this rate is a result of an effective recognition and reward system. After all, why would the associates be willing to submit quality-related ideas if there were nothing in it for them?

And this is not an isolated example. Wainwright has been encouraging, and getting, ideas from associates for years. Between September 1991 and September 1993, the number of these ideas submitted annually kept rising (Exhibit 7-6). In September 1991, there were 482; by September 1992, almost 2,500; by September 1993, over 4,150; and for 1994, the goal was 4,400. The fact that the associates reached their suggestion implementation goal by 1993 speaks well for their ability to continue this trend. In addition, these ideas have helped account for the gross profit-sales increases that almost doubled between 1991 and 1994 and are projected to

Exhibit 7-6. Suggestion implementation rate at Wainwright Industries.

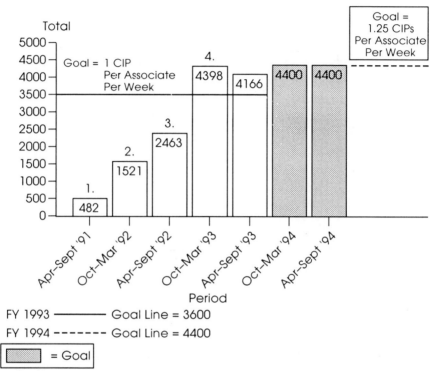

Courtesy: Wainwright Industries.

increase another 40 percent by 1996 (Exhibit 7-7). Clearly the associates at Wainwright are committed to the company's quality efforts.

American Capital Companies Shareholder Services (ACCESS)

At ACCESS, quality and operational results are similar to those at Wainwright, and the feedback shows that things are getting increasingly better. Exhibit 7-8 reports error rates for monetary transactions, nonmonetary transactions, and correspondence accuracy. In the case of both monetary and nonmonetary transactions, over a five-year period there has been an 80 percent reduction in mistakes; in the case of correspondence, the reduction has been around

Exhibit 7-7. Fiscal year gross profit trend at Wainwright Industries.

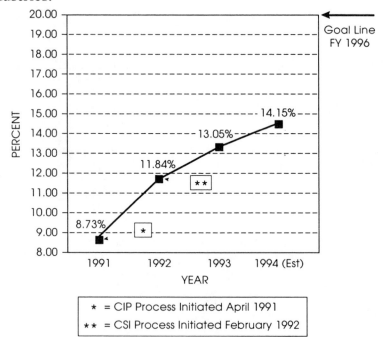

Courtesy: Wainwright Industries.

75 percent over the previous twelve quarters. These results clearly illustrate that ACCESS associates are committed to the quality effort, and there is every reason to believe that the organization's reward and recognition system is working well.

Phelps County Bank

Phelps's measures to evaluate progress are broken into two categories: internal and external. Internally the bank measures productivity by dividing costs per million dollars of assets per day. In 1991 salaries and benefit expense per million dollars of assets per day was $63.08; by 1993 this had been reduced to $56.19, a 13 percent improvement in two years, which equated to a cost reduction of $255,131 in this last year. Another measure is assets per employee. During this two-year period the bank increased its assets from

Exhibit 7-8. Quality results at American Capital Companies Shareholder Services, Inc.

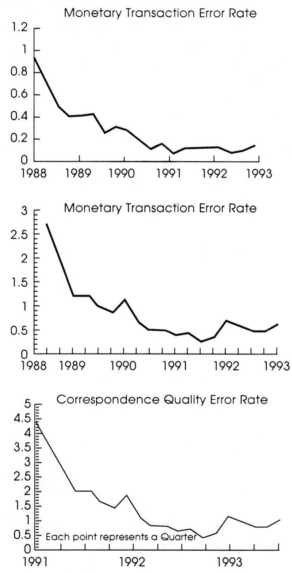

$1.65 million to $1.91 million per employee—an improvement of 16 percent, which contrasts favorably with similar banks, which had an average increase of only 11 percent. A third internal measure is how well the bank complies with safety and soundness standards and regulatory laws, as viewed by the bank examiners. In each of the past five years Phelps has received the highest regulatory ratings given.

Externally, Phelps measures performance by comparing its growth of deposits, loans, and assets against this growth by two prime competitors and by comparing its return on investment against a national peer group. Since 1986 Phelps's share of deposits, compared to those of its three competitors, has increased from 33 percent to 39 percent; its market share of loans has risen from 29 percent to 39 percent; and its market share of assets has increased from 32 percent of total assets held by the three banks to 39 percent. As a result, Phelps, which was the smallest of the three banks in assets, is now the largest. And its return on investment over the past five years has averaged 18.08 percent compared to 13.04 percent for banks of similar size in nonmetropolitan areas. The bank's recognition and reward system is undoubtedly working very well.

Develop Your Own Recognition and Reward System

There are a number of key steps to consider in developing the recognition and reward system that will work best in your organization. Remember that this step may take three or four years to implement fully; you are likely to be continually modifying the system and making changes. Additionally, the first couple of months with the system may generate significant results, followed by a sharp drop in performance as the newness wears off and associates begin losing their enthusiasm. It may be necessary to monitor what is working and what is not and make changes as you go along. In particular, it is important not to overemphasize money because it is extremely difficult to reduce financial awards without suffering a loss of support from the associates. So start slowly, design a system that encourages participation, and remember that psychological rewards, such as a thank-you note or a picture on the wall for the Departmental Employee of the Month, often have more long-lasting value than a $500 check. It is also important to get everyone involved by making it possible for them to earn recognition and rewards.

Finally, it is critical to monitor performance, so you can judge how well the system is working. You can talk to associates and get their feedback; look at the number of suggestions that are submitted each month; review how well the quality teams are implementing new ideas; and monitor key performance areas such as cycle time, error rate, and customer satisfaction. These steps can help you identify breakdowns in the system and begin taking corrective action.

In carrying out these steps, the following worksheet provides some useful guiding questions. Be sure to share these with those who are helping you design the recognition and reward system. Your decisions will have a great impact on the willingness of the associates to strive for continuous improvement.

Developing an Effective Recognition and Reward System

1. Who will design the recognition and reward system? Will there be representation from throughout the organization? If not, why not?

2. What forms of recognition and rewards will be given to the personnel?

3. What will the associates have to do to qualify for recognition and/or rewards? Will everyone have an opportunity to participate in the system? If not, why not?

4. How will we evaluate the results of the recognition and reward system? What measures will be used? How often will this be done? If there are problems, what action(s) will be taken?

8

Maintain Continuous Improvement—Don't Ever Stop Getting Better!

One of the primary reasons that TQM efforts fail is that the enterprise does not improve. Once the company reaches its initial quality goals, TQM interest wanes. As a result, competitors start to close the quality gap, and the benefit of the company's TQM program proves to be short-lived. One of the most effective ways of preventing this is through the use of a well-formulated continuous improvement (CI) program.

At the heart of every CI program is a carefully crafted reward and recognition system. Associates have to believe that their efforts are being continually rewarded. When this does not happen, the TQM effort begins to flounder. In sidestepping this problem and maintaining the CI momentum, four steps are of paramount importance:

First	Develop quantitative measures, such as percentages, costs, revenues, time, or dollars, so that you know the status of your quality efforts and do not look at mere anecdotal data as truth.
Second	Use benchmarking and similar approaches to help generate creative, unique solutions and learn how to think "outside the box," by looking at problems in new ways.
Third	Focus on achieving small, incremental improvements in quality, as opposed to trying for large advances that come as a result of occasional major

breakthroughs, because it is more important to have continual improvement than the starts and stops that characterize these giant, periodic increases.

Fourth   Working within the three previous guidelines, develop a CI system that will work best for your own organization.

Determine How Well You Are Doing

It is important to quantify your quality progress whenever possible so that you know how well you are doing and can plan your next move. This step may require a good deal of courage, since it means a willingness to accept the fact that the numbers may indicate slippage and you will have to admit the need for change. We will briefly look at the concept of 6 sigma, and then consider examples of how some companies go about determining how well they are doing.

Decide How to Compute Your Error Rate

Sigma is a term used to describe error rates. Companies such as Motorola have made the term *6 sigma* famous because their goal is to drive down their failure rates to the point at which they reach the 6 sigma level.

Exhibit 8-1 provides a graphic illustration of quality improvement at increasing levels of sigma. Note that at 3 sigma, the error rate is 66,810 parts per million (ppm), or 6.7 percent. At 4 sigma, the number of errors drops to 6,210 ppm, or less than 1 percent. At 5 sigma, there are 233 errors per million, and at 6 sigma there are only 3.4 errors per million. Notice also that in moving from 3 to 4 sigma, quality improves by a factor of 10. Between 4 and 5 sigma, the improvement factor is 30, and between 5 and 6 sigma the factor is 70. So at 6 sigma there are virtually no mistakes being made.

To put this information in a more practical light, Exhibit 8-2 applies these ideas to selected activities of average and best-in-class companies. It shows that many average companies operate at 4

Exhibit 8-1. Quality improvement at increasing levels of sigma.

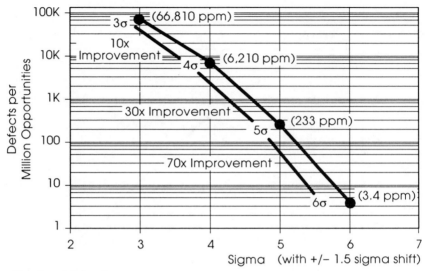

Courtesy: Motorola.

sigma, while best-in-class organizations are at the 6 sigma level. For example, at the time Exhibit 8-2 was constructed, Internal Revenue Service tax advisers were giving 140,000 incorrect answers per 1 million responses (2 sigma), while airlines lost 4,000 pieces of luggage per 1 million shipped (4 sigma) but had a flight fatality rate of less than 1 for every 2 million flights (6 + sigma).

In determining your own organization's error rates (or sigma), one of the biggest problems is determining how to compute the number of opportunities for mistakes. For example, if your company is producing small motors and you manufacture 100 units without an error, how would you use the following formula to compute your error rate:

$$\frac{\text{Number of errors or defects}}{\text{Number of opportunities for mistakes}}$$

Obviously the numerator is zero, but what is the denominator? If there are two parts in the motor that must be screwed together, is this one opportunity for error? If the screw must be turned six times in order to lock it in, does this raise the number of

Exhibit 8-2. Quality performance among selected activities.

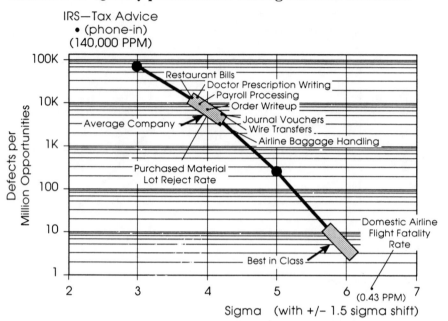

Courtesy: Motorola.

opportunities to six? Companies that measure error rates per million often spend a lot of time deciding how to determine the number of opportunities, and the outcome is often an arbitrary decision since there is no right answer. So if you decide to measure your error rate, you must also remember that there is some degree of arbitrary assignment.

Nevertheless, the idea of moving toward 6 sigma or some similar improvement strategy is important. And even if you are not interested in computing the failure rate per million opportunities, you must be willing to determine how well you are doing and what steps need to be taken to reduce the error or mistake rate. This is not very difficult to do as long as you get feedback and use Pareto analysis and/or cause-and-effect diagrams (see Chapter 5) to evaluate the results and decide where to go. In this way, you will be able to measure progress.

Measure Your Current Progress

There are a number of ways of measuring progress. Here are four case examples.

Wainwright Industries

Wainwright offers a good example of how to measure progress over time. Exhibit 8-3 provides some illustrations. Note that freight cost as a percentage of sales declined by 80 percent, loss prevention over a three-year period declined from over $92,000 to $13,041, and customer satisfaction rose consistently, almost reaching the desired level for the current year.

These figures clearly show continuous improvement. They also help Wainwright keep focused on key performance areas. If something were to go wrong, the company would see the turnaround and could begin making changes to correct the problem. These figures are also useful because they illustrate the data, thus making it easy to understand and, if necessary, act on the information.

Valley Hospital Medical Center

Valley provides another example of how to determine progress. In this case the hospital identified key areas in which it wanted to improve performance. These are indicated in Exhibit 8-4 as boxed information. For example, in the Emergency Room (ER) the hospital chose a number of areas for which it had baseline data and sought to improve performance. The same is true for the other four areas in the exhibit. A close look at select examples in the exhibit shows that Valley was successful in most of these areas:

- Waiting time in the ER declined below 20 minutes in six of the past seven months, although it reached a new high (22.1 minutes) in the previous month.
- The time to be seen by a physician declined from 27 minutes to as low as 12.6 minutes.
- Admission time dropped from 24.47 minutes to under 20 minutes.

Exhibit 8-3. Measuring progress at Wainwright Industries.

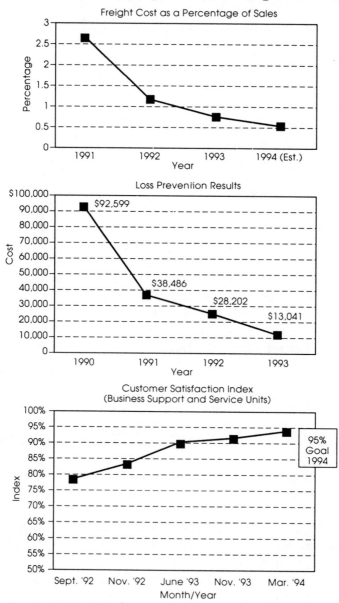

Courtesy: Wainwright Industries.

- Turnaround time needed to get reports to physicians dropped from 38 hours to under 30 during each of the past four months.
- Over 95 percent of inpatient laboratory tests were reported by 8 A.M. In recent months, a higher rate than previously.
- Mistakes (e.g., medication errors, patient falls) declined to an eight-month low.

This comparative approach is particularly helpful in determining out how well the hospital is improving quality because there is a baseline against which to measure performance, so Valley can keep comparing itself against this baseline. If it wants to raise the bar, it can choose the latest results to use as the new baseline. In either event, the hospital continually knows how well it is doing.

American Capital Companies Shareholder Services (ACCESS)

ACCESS uses a similar approach to Valley except that it does not establish a formal baseline for each activity and work against that one. Rather, it tries to improve quality by working better than previously. Exhibit 8-5 provides an example. Notice that there are eight factors being measured, and in most cases the results are getting continually better. For example, the percentage of team meetings that are being held is at the 98 + % level, and cost savings are way up over the past two years.

The important thing to draw from this example is the need to get constant feedback and use it for comparative purposes. If things start going wrong, ACCESS will be able to identify the trend quickly and start developing a response strategy. And although there are likely to be downturns or slippages along the way, these will be only brief aberrations as long as the organization keeps the focus on CI.

Mayport Naval Station

Mayport provides yet another good example of measuring progress for the purpose of ensuring CI. The naval station's Aviation Intermediate Maintenance Department (AIMD) was selected from all of these departments in the navy by the Navy Aviation Supply

(text continues on page 188)

Exhibit 8-4. Quality key processing at Valley Hospital Medical Center.

	1992		1993							
	November (partial month)	Dec.	Jan.	Feb.	March	Apr.	May	June	July	Aug.
ER Patient Flow										
Waiting time taken into ER (time 1)	21 min.	19 min.	20 min.	15 min.	13 min.	15 min.	17.54 min.	15.69	17.40	22.1
Seen by physician (time 2)	27 min.	31 min.	27 min.	31 min.	30 min.	17 min.	16.15 min.	16.49	12.60	17.0
Number of patients checked in	2330	2311	2316	2393	2667	3117	2530	2146	2615	2576
Leave w/o being seen	37	31	70	47	59	35	32	16	37	29
% of total seen	1.38	1.34	3.02	1.96	2.21	1.12	1.26	.75	1.41	1.13
Admissions										
Admits: total registration time (min.)	22.75	24.18	24.47	23.17	23.16	21.41	21.95	19.48	21.47	19.40

Outpatient: total registration time	23.66	20.85	26.08	15.70	14.51	15.45	14.48	13.30	14.46	17.28
Emergency: total registration time	19.63	18.72	17.77							
Outpatient imaging Number of reports	120	344	320	271	251	236	230	(Random Sample) 98	50	47
Report to physician	55%<24 hrs.	81%<24	66%<24	78%<24	80%<24	48%<24	66%<24	84%<24	100%<24	83%<24
Turnaround time (hours)	38 hrs.	28 hrs.	24 hrs.	23 hrs.	23 hrs.	34 hrs.	27 hrs.	26.5 hrs.	22.5 hrs.	28 hrs.
Inpatient lab testing Number of A.M. labs ordered	41,719	62,337	(started random sample) 7,743	9,175	9,110	7,488	7,817	7,417	8,027	6,420
Results by 8:00 A.M.	39,707	55,990	7,188	8,685	8,531	7,301	7,479	7,224	7,562	6,176
% of results by 8:00 A.M.	95%	90%	92.8%	94.7%	93.6%	97.5%	95.7%	97.4%	94.2%	96.2%
Nursing care Medication errors	11	10	17	14	26	17	26	18	17	14
Patient falls	16	17	26	18	19	20	27	17	22	14
Decubiti (hospital acquired)	3	2	2	1	1	3	4	1	1	-0-

Note: Boxed data are baseline data.
Courtesy: Valley Hospital Medical Center.

Exhibit 8-5. Continuous improvement at ACCESS, Inc.

Measurement	1990	1991	1992	Year to Date, 1993
Hours in team training	912	1,144	936	50
Percentage of team meetings held	78.6	79	99	98.2
Number of ideas generated	180	1,113	785	231
Percentage of certified ideas implemented	8	57	62	47
Cost savings from quality control team ideas	$2,884.16	$149,732.01	$186,766.61	$141,070.54
Hours saved by quality control team ideas	180.26	6,699.52	12,343.13	6,054.99
Number of cross-functional/level teams used	2	7	28	25
Percentage of teams (excluding quality teams) that are cross-functional/level in design	33	33	40	44

Courtesy: ACCESS, Inc.

Office to produce a video to inspire the rest of the fleet to get involved in finding innovative ways to increase productivity. Mayport's AIMD efforts saved the government over $8 million in a recent year, while providing better service to the fleet (Exhibit 8-6). By keeping track of such progress, CI continues to be a key area of consideration at Mayport.

Look Into Benchmarking

One of the problems that many organizations face when trying to implement a CI program is that they run out of good ideas for improvements. This is where benchmarking can be of value because it can help you "think outside the box." One way is to look at how jobs in the industry are done and see if improvements can

Exhibit 8-6. Improvements by employees in the Aviation Intermediate Maintenance Department, Mayport Naval Station.

Cost Savings Initiatives	Specifics	Savings in Dollars
Expanded intermediate-level repair capabilities	1. Engine compressor rotor repair	1. $3,613,376
	2. Center stabilator bushing repair	2. $875,000
	3. Avionics/weapons control panel test set	3. $755,000
	4. Pilot-assist modules	4. $250,000
	5. Scissors assembly repair	5. $86,000
	6. Consolidated Metcal program	6. $42,000
	7. Vibration analysis test set	7. $39,270
	8. Rotor brake manifold assembly repair	8. $27,387
	9. IFF/TACAN, microwave equip, temp measuring devices calibration	9. $24,000
Designed or manufactured new test equipment, tools, repair equipment	1. Main rotor head dampener manufacture	1. $476,500
	2. Fuel/oil line set manufacture	2. $329,938
	3. Engine compressor rotor locknut ratchet manufacture	3. $329,415
	4. Stabilizer actuator fixtures manufacture	4. $119,000
	5. Master caution panel test set	5. $104,900
	6. Blade fold control panel test set	6. $60,000
	7. Pitch lock actuator test bench fixtures	7. $53,460
Designed or developed new procedures	1. Main rotor head dampener accumulator repair	1. $1,610,700
	2. Antenna radome storage and packing	2. $80,000
	3. Floorboard panel repair	3. $48,050
Expanded authorized maintenance	1. Arresting gear repairs	1. $25,500
	2. Arresting gear engine upgrades	2. $20,000
Total savings		$8,969,496

Courtesy: Mayport Naval Station.

be made in terms of both time and/or output. An excellent example is provided by Globe Metallurgical.

After the union walked out of the plant and management and a small number of associates were left to run operations, Globe began trying to improve efficiency by brainstorming and thinking outside the box. How could work be done better and less expensively? One of the jobs in the plant required workers to break up metal after it had set in the cooling molds. They then passed the metal over a grid, where someone would break it up manually. As the metal fell through the grid, it landed in containers, which were then transported by forklift to the bulk storage area.

One day the associates in the grid area came up with a new idea. Why break up the metal and drop it into containers? Why not simply dump it directly from the mold into a truck, which would then haul it away? The drop from the mold to the truck should be sufficient to break up the metal. The company tried the idea and it worked, saving more than $300,000 a year in salaries and expenses and creating a new way of doing this job throughout the industry.

Study the Jobs and the Processes

In benchmarking, it is important to study both the job and the processes that are used in doing the work. Sometimes benchmarking is useful in determining how a job can be done better or faster. However, quite often the success of the analysis focuses most heavily on changing the process used in getting the work done. As you read about the following two award-winning companies that are doing an excellent job of benchmarking, consider whether they offer ideas that you can emulate.

AIL Systems

AIL has a well-developed approach to benchmarking that not only explains what benchmarking is all about, but how it can be implemented. At the heart of the process is the idea of continuously trying to improve operations. The company defines benchmarking as:

> The continuous process of measuring AIL's performance (products, services, and practices) against "Best in Class" companies to determine how they achieve those performance levels, and then using the information as a basis for AIL's own targets, strategies, and implementation.

The key word in the definition is "continuous" because only by benchmarking on an ongoing basis is the organization able to maintain best-in-class performance. Moreover, benchmarking focuses on a wide number of areas including products, services, methods of manufacture, operating procedures, processes, and policies. And AIL does not look at just its major competitors to find out how things can be done better. The company benchmarks best practices from *any* industry. This is made clear by the company's main reasons for benchmarking: (1) to become more competitive by reducing cycle time from concept to finished product and to achieve best-in-class performance, (2) to improve processes that are critical to operations, (3) to take advantage of best commercial practices to improve processes, (4) to reduce operational expenses, and (5) to help achieve the continuous improvement objectives of AIL 2000. The approach used in benchmarking is a generic one that has been modified to fit AIL's needs. In all, there are six steps:

1. The process or activity to be benchmarked is determined, those who will be involved in the benchmarking are identified, and a flow chart of how the work is being done currently is constructed.
2. Research is conducted to find out what is currently known about the process or activity that is being benchmarked, including checking with in-house experts and using library sources, customer surveys, and industry publications.
3. Additional data is collected on the benchmarked process or activity through visits to other companies, interviews, and questionnaires.
4. The findings are evaluated and decisions are made regarding how to use the information.
5. The data are applied and adapted to the benchmarked process or activity.
6. The changes are institutionalized and made part of the ongoing operating process.

AIL provides a good example of how to tap available benchmarking sources. And many of them are in the public domain. The information can be obtained by going to the library, looking through professional and trade association data, and getting information from the Department of Commerce. Additionally, readily available sources include suppliers and customers. And if more information is needed, it is often possible to get it through telephone surveys, mail surveys, and on-site visits to other organizations. (Keep in mind, however, that the latter are more interested in sharing information rather than just giving it away. So your company should be prepared to give the other company some information about your approaches to doing things. In this way, both of you end up getting benchmarking information.)

In AIL's case, its benchmarking efforts have resulted in continuous improvement in a number of areas including reduced defect rates, lower costs for rework and repair, reduced recurrence rate of material review, a lower ratio of electrical inspection hours to electrical assembly hours, and increased first-pass yield. Exhibit 8-7 provides information related to the latter.

In addition, the company's initiatives in the material control area have led to a 93 percent reduction in the time required to pull a kit, and a 98 percent reduction in the time required to issue a replacement part to manufacturing. The company has also developed a process with its office supplies vendor to provide just-in-time inventory, thus reducing storage space and cutting costs. Other examples of the effect of its benchmarking efforts include:

1. The company's accident rate is now less than 20 percent of the averages reported by the Bureau of Labor Statistics, and fire insurance premiums are 15 percent of the base rate expected for a facility of its size and type.
2. The value-added sales per staff member are $2.83 for every dollar of payroll spent, which is 7 percent more favorable than the industry average of $2.64.
3. Turnaround time in the instrument resources area has been reduced by 27 percent.
4. Cycle time from receipt of a purchase requisition to placement of purchase order has been reduced by 60 percent.
5. Response to customer requests for quotes has been reduced from seventy days down to twenty days.

Exhibit 8-7. Some continuous improvement results at AIL.

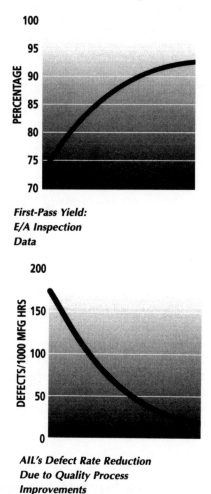

First-Pass Yield:
E/A Inspection
Data

AIL's Defect Rate Reduction
Due to Quality Process
Improvements

6. The average age of accounts receivable has been cut in half, and computer response time has been reduced by 75 percent.

Wainwright Industries

Benchmarking is particularly helpful in showing how well you are doing against the best in your class. It is also possible to include other groups in the analysis, so that you are comparing yourself against competitors (or the industry mean or median) as well as the industry benchmark. Wainwright recently did this for its main manufacturing operations and found the following:

Category	Current Wainwright Rating (%)	Industry Median (%)	Industry Benchmark (%)
Manufacturing cycle time reduction	99.88	62	95
Product development cycle time reduction	70	50	81
5-year productivity improvement	260	38.4	363
5-year cost reduction	35	30	71

These data show that the company is doing a very good job when compared to the median performance in the industry. The company is also doing well in reducing manufacturing cycle time. However, in the other areas, especially overall cost reduction, the industry benchmark is much better than that of the company, and continuous improvement is needed.

Focus on Continuous Small Improvements

Continuous improvement relies on two developments: consistent, incremental gains and occasional innovation. While the latter is helpful, TQM-driven organizations give it less emphasis because it is unpredictable and nonincremental, an idea illustrated in Exhibit 8-8, in which the vertical lines show the result of innovation and the upwardly sloping lines reflect the effects of consistent, incremental gains. Clearly, if the sloping lines were eliminated, overall improvement would drop sharply. Innovation is important, but it

Exhibit 8-8. Innovation and constant improvement at Zytec Corporation.

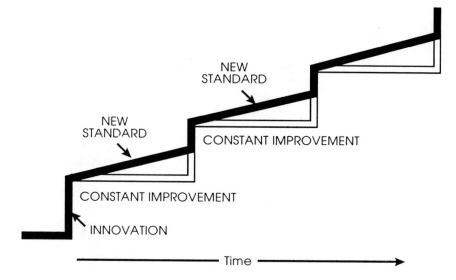

Source: Zytec Corporation. Used by permission.

cannot be relied on for day-to-day quality improvements. The organization may encounter a sharp increase in productivity in a particular area because of a major quality-related breakthrough, but such developments will occur infrequently, and if the enterprise relies on innovation for continuous improvement, progress will be slow.

The reason for focusing on small improvements is illustrated in Exhibit 8-9, where constant improvement and innovation are contrasted. Some of the main differences that favor constant improvement are the long-term effect of this incremental approach, the gradual (as opposed to abrupt) change that takes place, and the fact that everyone is involved in the process.

Get Teams Involved in the Process

Many organizations create teams to help them maintain their CI emphasis. A good example is Baptist Hospital of Miami.

Exhibit 8-9. Constant improvement and innovation at Zytec Corporation: a comparison.

Characteristic	Constant Improvement	Innovation
Effect	Long term and long lasting but undramatic	Short term but dramatic
Pace	Small steps	Big steps
Time frame	Continuous and incremental	Intermittent and nonincremental
Change	Gradual and constant	Abrupt and volatile
Involvement	Everybody	A few selected "champions"
Approach	Collectivism, group efforts, systems	Rugged individualism, ideas and efforts generated by one person
Mode	Maintenance and improvement	Scrap and rebuild
Spark	Conventional know-how and state of the art	Technological breakthroughs, new inventions, new theories
Practical requirements	Little investigation, great effort to maintain improvement	Large investigation, little effort to maintain improvement
Effort orientation	People	Technology
Evaluation criteria	Process and efforts for better results	Results for profit
Advantage	Works well in slow-growth economy	Better suited to fast-growth economy

Courtesy: Zytec Corporation. Used by permission.

Baptist Hospital of Miami

Baptist has had a CI initiative that involves the wide use of CI teams. These multidisciplinary groups use the types of tools and techniques described in Chapter 5: Pareto analysis, cause-and-effect diagrams, and brainstorming. Examples of these teams and their expected outcomes include:

Continuous Improvement Teams	Expected Outcomes
Emergency Department (ED) opportunities	Reduce total throughput time of all ED patients.
Records and film retrieval	Review the existing system for off-site storage and retrieval of medical records and x-ray film, and recommend solutions that will result in short-term and long-term improvements.
Inventory controllers	Reduce inventory and achieve operational efficiency by streamlining the process for replenishing supplies in the satellite inventory system.
Admission/discharge system	Improve the patient through the admission and discharge process.
Transcultural enhancement	Develop transcultural modalities to more appropriately meet the needs of the diverse guest/community population.
International services	Define and develop a formal international services program.
Outpatient rehabilitation patient scheduling	Improve the overall effectiveness of the scheduling process in a cost-efficient manner.

Patient parking in the southeast quadrant	Provide an efficient, cost-effective, convenient service while ensuring customer satisfaction and safety.
Continuous improvement informers	Develop a formal method for collecting and disseminating continuous improvement information to any group(s) that may need or benefit from this information.
Clinical information retrieval	Improve the timeliness of availability of medical records so that information may be retrieved in the most efficient manner permitted.

Each team develops its own approach to addressing problems in its area. For example, the ED redesign CI team has been charged with reviewing and reengineering all emergency services at the hospital. This effort obviously is going to take a great deal of time because the team will have to look at a number of different areas. Prior to the appointment of the committee, a consulting team had been hired to assess the day-to-day operations of the ED's activities. The CI team evaluated the findings of the consultants and used them as the basis for establishing a primary focus. The consultants' recommendations are presented in Exhibit 8-10 and provide some insights regarding the information with which the team began its efforts.

As the CI team began addressing the various problems, it relied heavily on brainstorming, flowcharting, and fishbone diagrams. For example, the team decided to address the problem of waiting time in the treatment area before a disposition decision was made. After brainstorming and constructing a cause-and-effect diagram, the group identified "need for improved communication" as a key area that needed to be addressed. Some of the reasons for this problem included the need for better interpersonal

Exhibit 8-10. Consultants' recommendations regarding day-to-day operations of the Emergency Department: Baptist Hospital of Miami.

Situation	Recommendation	Expected Outcome	Method of Evaluation
Patient processing/ placement delays	Implement hybrid observation unit/ Private Medical Doctor Service	Significant decrease in processing of patients	Turnaround time for patients
Inconsistent triage system/coverage	Adherence to formalized triage process	Marked improvement in classification/ placement of patient	Entry/triage/ placement disposition times
Inadequate systems for patient intake, processing and status	Implement patient status board/re-organization of paper flow	Marked improvement in ability to place/monitor patient status	Patient turnaround times
Inconsistent shift authority and accountability roles	Implement resource management nurse positions	Marked improvement in shift management	Physician/nursing/ technican surveys and interviews
Problematic congestion/location of administrative functions	Relocation of medical records/billing/ administrative functions	Reduce confusion for patients/improved registration process	Patient surveys and registration processing times
Inadequate physical configuration of nursing workstation	Redesign workstation to improve staff circulation	Improved workspace and circulation of staff	Patient and staff satisfaction
Delays in patient flow	Implement modified primary nursing team concept	Seamless patient care/decreased waiting times for ancillary services	Patient satisfaction/improved communications in waiting and treatment areas/ increased security for patients, staff, and visitors
Inadequate security at department entry	Place un-uniformed security at entry	Enhanced patient reception and information assistance status	Patient satisfaction/improved communications in waiting and treatment areas/ increased security for patients, staff, and visitors

(continues)

Exhibit 8-10. *(Continued)*

Situation	Recommendation	Expected Outcome	Method of Evaluation
Lack of adequate visitor control	Enforce visitor policy for treatment area; Station ununiformed security in reception area to assist with communication between waiting and treatment areas	Improved workflows/ increased security staff and patients/decreased staff frustration	Patient flow studies/patient satisfaction surveys/ staff surveys and incident reports
Physically ill patients sitting in entry and waiting areas of department	Designate subwaiting area for minor care patients and patients awaiting treatment room placement	Improved overall patient flow/ improved patient privacy and satisfaction	Patient flow studies/patient satisfaction surveys

Courtesy: Baptist Hospital of Miami.

relations; improved communication between departments; better telephone communication; more effective written communication; improved communication among the ED staff, the patient, and the family; and better communication of the patient's status. In response, the team instituted a number of changes including:

- Increasing the number of phone lines in the treatment room
- Revising the ED patient survey so as to better identify trends
- Creating a dedicated ED physician/ambulance parking area
- Reformatting of existing data for easier retrieval to measure outcome
- Standardizing the placement of charts
- Allocating a patient representative in the treatment area
- Reevaluating staffing requirements for the department as reengineering occurs

The CI team is continuing its efforts along these same lines. And they are tracking progress, so that they know what has been accomplished, how well it has turned out, and what now needs to be done. You can use this same type of approach in ensuring that your organization does not lose its determination for continuous improvement.

Develop Your Own System for Continuous Improvement

In developing your own system for CI, keep four points in mind:

1. Be sure the system is tailor-made for your organization. The examples provided in this chapter should help in pinpointing steps for you to take, but each enterprise needs to develop an approach that fits its own specific demands.
2. Because an effective CI system is heavily databased, it is important to collect information continually on all key areas and carefully chart progress. In this way you know how well you are doing and where improvements can and should be made.
3. Involve everyone in the process. In the beginning you are likely to have only a few CI teams, but as progress is made and you begin getting further into the quality journey, create more teams and eventually get everyone involved in the process.
4. Remember that one of the main determinants to the success of every effort is an effective recognition and reward system. If you don't reward your associates, they are not going to sustain their support for the quality effort.

The following worksheet draws together some of this information and should be particularly useful to you in formulating an effective CI strategy.

Designing a Continuous Improvement Program

1. What are the key performance areas that ultimately determine the success of our organization? Identify them.

2. For each of the key performance areas, how will we gather data and track progress? What role will Q teams play?

3. How will we use benchmarking or some similar approach to generate improvement ideas? What procedures will we use in implementing this process?

4. How will we maintain the focus on continuous improvement? What types of recognition or reward system will we use in doing this?

Epilogue

There are a number of steps to take in instituting quality in your organization. Now that you are nearly finished reading this book, this is a good time to recap these ideas in the form of useful guidelines. Seven points are of primary importance:

1. Develop a quality focus by creating a vision and/or mission statement. This step may not be fully completed until you are well into the quality journey, but start with at least an initial focus or statement that serves as a point of reference.
2. Identify your customer needs—those of both internal and external customers. This step requires gathering information through surveys and interviews.
3. Design an organization structure that helps implement your quality-driven strategy.
4. Train associates in the necessary tools and techniques: checksheets, Pareto charts, cause-and-effect diagrams, and brainstorming. Be sure to use only the tools that are useful to your organization. Forget the rest.
5. Give and get feedback from both internal and external customers. This feedback can take a variety of forms and should be designed to meet the unique needs of your customers.
6. Develop an effective recognition and reward system. The focus should be on rewards that maintain continuous improvement efforts and should not be overly reliant on financial rewards.
7. Create the necessary climate for maintaining continuous improvement efforts. This means reviewing the other six guidelines and using this information to keep the quality momentum.

A good way of remembering this last point is provided by Zytec, one of the companies interviewed for this book and one of leading small manufacturers in America. The company uses the following story to help emphasize the continuous improvement challenge, and it is one worth remembering:

> Every morning in Africa,
>   a gazelle wakes up.
> It knows it must outrun
>   the fastest lion
>   or it will be killed.
>
> Every morning in Africa,
>   a lion wakes up.
> It knows it must run faster
>   than the slowest gazelle
>   or it will starve.
>
> It doesn't matter whether
> you're a lion or a gazelle—
>   when the sun comes up,
>   you'd better be running.

Bibliography

A number of other books can complement this one and help you in designing and implementing a TQM program quickly and efficiently. Here are some that I have found to be of particular value.

Andrews, Dorine C., and Susan K. Stalick. *Business Reengineering: The Survival Guide*. Englewood Cliffs, N.J.: Yourdon Press, 1994. For organizations looking into reengineering their processes as part of the TQM effort, this book provides some excellent insight into how to prepare for reengineering and then implement it properly.

Berry, Thomas H. *Managing the Total Quality Management Transformation*. New York: McGraw-Hill, 1991. Particularly effective in explaining how to organize the TQM effort through the use of quality planning, formation of a quality department and quality teams, and how to sustain the effort through the use of continuous improvement ideas.

Bounds, Greg, Lyle Yorks, Mel Adams, and Gipsie Ranney. *Beyond Total Quality Management: Toward the Emerging Paradigm*. New York: McGraw-Hill, 1994. Designed primarily as a college textbook but also an excellent resource for those wanting to learn about TQM and how to implement it in their organization. It covers in depth all of the key areas that are critical to the effort: changing the culture, identifying management's role, identifying and measuring customer value, organizing the process, and controlling the overall effort.

Bowles, Jerry, and Joshua Hammond. *Beyond Quality: How 50 Winning Companies Use Continuous Improvement*. New York: G. P. Putnam's Sons, 1991. Replete with stories and examples of how some of the best organizations worldwide use continuous improvement ideas. The material is presented in the form of topic areas, not company stories, so it is easy to understand the basic lessons that are being discussed.

Camp, Robert C. *Benchmarking: The Search for Industry Best Practices That Lead to Superior Performance.* Milwaukee: Quality Press, 1989. Long the leader in the area of benchmarking, this book provides a detailed discussion of the steps in the process and offers a wide array of guidelines and suggestions for using benchmarking in any organization.

Champy, James. *Reengineering Management: The Mandate for New Leadership.* New York: Harper Business, 1995. A follow-on to *Reengineering the Corporation* (New York: Harper Business, 1993), which Champy coauthored with Michael Hammer. The first book emphasized the importance of reengineering operational processes. This one focuses on the changes that must take place in the management processes—mobilizing, enabling, defining, measuring, and communicating—in order to achieve a business culture that enables a continuous process of reengineering.

Cocheu, Ted. *Making Quality Happen: How Training Can Turn Strategy Into Real Improvement.* San Francisco: Jossey-Bass, 1993. Helps reinforce many of the critical areas of TQM, including the need to build a leadership foundation, gain understanding and commitment throughout the organization, implement the overall system, empower improvement teams, and create a learning organization.

Davenport, Thomas H. *Process Innovation: Reengineering Work Through Information Technology.* Boston: Harvard Business School Press, 1993. Explains how to carry out process innovation, an approach that fuses information technology and human resources management for the purpose of improving business performance, offering some excellent ideas that can be made part of the TQM change process.

Dobyns, Lloyd, and Clare Crawford-Mason. *Quality or Else: The Revolution in World Business.* Boston: Houghton Mifflin, 1991. A companion to the IBM-funded PBS series of the same name, this is an excellent initial resource in gaining an understanding of why quality is so important and what is being done about it worldwide.

Fisher, Donald D. *Measuring Up to the Baldrige: A Quick & Easy Self-*

Assessment Guide for Organizations of All Sizes. New York: AMACOM Books, 1994. Offers an excellent introduction to how an organization can apply the Baldrige criteria to its own operations, including how to evaluate and score company performance in all critical areas.

Gale, Bradley T. *Managing Customer Value: Creating Quality and Service That Customers Can See.* New York: Free Press, 1994. Particularly good for those who want to learn more about how to improve customer satisfaction through the use of such techniques as creating power brands, conducting customer value analysis, and achieving quality service.

Harrington, H. James. *Total Improvement Management: The Next Generation of Performance Improvement.* New York: McGraw-Hill, 1995. Focuses on continuous improvement and ways to use this idea to stay ahead in the global marketplace. Primary attention is given to showing how businesses can optimize their use of resources by blending elements of TQM, total productivity management, total cost management, total resource management, total technolgoy management, and total business management methodologies.

Harrison, Alan. *Just-in-Time Manufacturing in Perspective.* Englewood Cliffs, N.J.: Prentice-Hall, 1992. Provides a series of very useful ideas regarding how to incorporate just-in-time inventory into manufacturing operations by focusing on such key areas as suppliers, maintenance, push and pull scheduling, and implementation.

Hart, Christopher W. L., and Christopher E. Bogan. *The Baldrige: What Is It, How It's Won, How to Use It to Improve Quality in Your Company.* New York: McGraw-Hill, 1992. Describes the Baldrige award, identifies and discusses seven key pillars that provide the basis for effective quality, and offers executive exercises that are designed to reinforce these concepts.

Hinton, Tom, and Wini Schaeffer. *Customer-Focused Quality: What to Do on Monday Morning.* Englewood Cliffs, N.J.: Prentice-Hall, 1994. Emphasizes the importance of developing a quality focus by getting feedback from both internal and external customers and by using this information to educate and train associates, benchmark, lead by example, and champion quality.

Hodgetts, Richard M. *Blueprints for Continuous Improvement: Lessons*

From the Baldrige Winners. New York: American Management Association, 1993. Provides insights and guidelines regarding the steps employed by organizations that have won the Baldrige and offers practical suggestions for applying these ideas.

Hoffherr, Glen D., John W. Moran, and Gerald Nadler. *Breakthrough Thinking in Total Quality Management.* Englewood Cliffs, N.J.: Prentice-Hall, 1994. Focuses on the basics of TQM philosophies and how to use breakthrough thinking to design and implement a successful program.

Roberts, Harry V., and Bernard F. Sergesketter. *Quality Is Personal: A Foundation for Total Quality Management.* New York: Free Press, 1993. Focuses on getting personnel to commit to the TQM process by not just participating but also developing personal quality checklists that will help to bring about small, incremental improvements as well as to promote continuous improvement.

Sashkin, Marshall, and Kenneth J. Kiser. *Putting Total Quality Management to Work.* San Francisco: Berrett-Koehler Publishers, 1993. Helps explain the roots of TQM and some of the initial steps that should be taken in instituting a total quality program and maintaining the momentum.

Schmidt, Warren H., and Jerome P. Finnigan. *The Race Without a Finish Line.* San Francisco: Jossey-Bass, 1992. Provides useful ideas regarding starting points for a TQM effort and guidelines for implementation, including such areas as organizational roles, TQM tools, reward systems, and feedback systems.

Schmidt, Warren H., and Jerome P. Finnigan. *TQM Manager: A Practical Guide for Managing in a Total Quality Organization.* San Francisco: Jossey-Bass, 1993. A hands-on offering that provides useful guidelines regarding what managers need to know about TQM, how they can master the necessary TQM competencies, and ways in which they can sharpen their TQM skills.

Schonberger, Richard J. *Building a Chain of Customers.* New York: Free Press, 1990. Schonberger was one of the first writers to describe Japanese manufacturing techniques and in this book goes a step further, explaining how to keep the focus on the

customer, reduce waste, market effectively, and develop a
best-in-class company.

Spendolini, Michael J. *The Benchmarking Book.* New York: AMA-
COM, 1994. A detailed, comprehensive approach to benchmarking products, services, and work processes for any
organization. An excellent source for the basics of benchmarking.

Index